The *Complete* Guide to
Beading Techniques

Photo by Myra Nunley

Jane Davis

Published by

**krause
publications**

700 East State Street • Iola, WI 54990-0001
715/445-2214 • FAX: 715/445-4087   www.krause.com

Please call or write for our free catalog of publications. Our toll-free number to place an order or
obtain a free catalog is 800-258-0929 or please use our regular business telephone 715-445-2214
for editorial comment and further information.

Library of Congress Catalog Number 00-110072
ISBN 0-87341-967-7

Unless otherwise noted, all photography by Ken Keyes.
All illustrations by Jane Davis.

Dedication

I dedicate this work to my mother, Marit Allgood Powell, who has always encouraged my many artistic endeavors since childhood. Thank you Mom. I love you.

Acknowledgments

Thank you and many warm thoughts to Sylvia Sur for pre-editing my text, especially for setting up the beginning organization of the patterns, the technical re-write of Chapters 5, 7, and 8, and the thread chart and information on beads in Chapter 1. This book would have fallen far short of its title without you.

Thank you to Ken Keyes Photography for the great photos that make this book a cut above.

Thank you to Carole Tripp of Creative Castle for the use of your store, your answers to all of my beading questions, moral support, and mostly for our wonderful friendship.

Thank you to Roger Tripp for dragging the slide projector out of your closet so I could preview the slides, and for carting miscellaneous beading items to your office so I could pick them up.

Thank you to Amy Tincher-Durik for your patience and understanding and your wonderful work on this book.

Thank you to all of the bead artists who have lent me their beautiful beadwork to photograph or sent me slides to include in this book. Your work beautifies these pages.

Thank you most of all to Rich, Jeff, Andrew, and Jonathan, who at times were strained but still supported my efforts, when this book spread throughout the house and put activities on hold so I could get it done and do it well.

In memory of Lynn Langford. Life is short, so make the most of it, and spread as much kindness as you can along the way.

Photo of beaded angel used with permission from *Art of Seed Beading*, by Elizabeth Gourley, Jane Davis, and Ellen Talbott, Sterling Publishing, N.Y., N.Y., 1999.

Table of Contents

Detail of the antique serving tray on page 107.

This antique steel-cut bag from France still shows the blue coating on the metal-faceted beads, although much of it has rusted or begun to flake away.

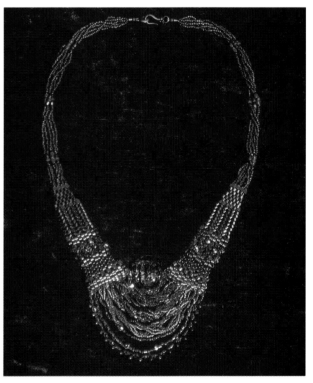

Ocean Waves, designed and stitched by Jane Davis. The use of various beading stitches adds texture to this piece.

Introduction

I was drawn to beadwork after seeing some amulet bags created by my friend Elizabeth Gourley and pulling out a treasured "some day I want to do this" article from 1986 on bead knitting by Alice Korach (the current editor of *Bead & Button Magazine*). Bead knitting was my first interest, and I searched out bead stores, magazine articles, and anything I could find to learn more. From there I progressed to peyote stitch and brick stitch. The first class I taught was the brick stitch Ladybug Box on page 36. I was extremely nervous at that first class, being very uncomfortable "on stage." But, my students were very gracious, and I'm still beading and teaching classes at Creative Castle in Newbury Park, California. During the same time period I entered a bead contest, and was amazed when my piece, Ocean Artisan, tied for the third place award. I was even more surprised when it was chosen for the cover of the companion book, *The Sea*. Since then, Liz Gourley, her twin sister Ellen Talbott, and I wrote *Art of Seed Beading*, and I have self-published three other beading books. I love all fine arts and crafts and find that my art background always helps with composition and color decisions.

This book is a result of my desire to try every possible handwork technique using beads. I have tried to make it as comprehensive as I could, all the time knowing it would be impossible to corral the ever-growing and ever-changing world of beads into one book. It is also my personal view of beading, which is a vast and varied creative field, with many different ways of doing the same thing. Because of this, I think of this book more as a sampling of beadwork, and so I have explained most techniques using a small sample first. A complete and creative project follows each how-to section. Several of the techniques, such as knitting, crochet, and tatting, assume the reader already has a skilled knowledge of the process, and so those sections do not cover the basics of that technique, but only how to use it incorporating beads. The final project, in Chapter 19, is a composite sampler using many of the techniques from the book. Throughout the book you will also find photos of beautiful antique beadwork and inspiring work of contemporary artists.

I hope you enjoy the projects in this book as much as I have enjoyed creating them.

Jane Davis

How to Use This Book

I wrote this book as both a reference and a project book. Before beginning a project in an unfamiliar technique, look over Chapter 1, The Basics, and then familiarize yourself with the new technique by making the learning sample that is provided before each project. For each sample, feel free to choose the color of beads and thread of your liking, unless otherwise noted. You can use these samples for small decorative projects like the ones shown here, or in Chapter 19, The Sampler, you can combine the learning samples into a sampler wall hanging.

The learning samples throughout the book can be used for a variety of small projects.

Chapter 1

The Basics

This chapter describes and illustrates the basic tools required for beadwork. Special tools such as bead looms are illustrated at the beginning of the chapters in which you learn how to use them with beads.

Beads

Technically, anything with a hole can be used as a bead. Most of the projects in this book use two types of glass beads, seed beads and Delica beads, but there are also other types available.

Seed beads are shaped like doughnuts and range from the tiny, antique size 24 beads used for miniature detail in projects, to the 1/8-inch tall by almost 3/16-inch wide size 6 beads used in the knitted pillow and right-angle weave basket projects (on pages 76 and 68, respectively). The higher the number, the smaller the bead.

Because of their curved sides, seed beads are well suited for techniques where the beads are arranged diagonally or at right angles, such as knitting, crochet, right-angle weave, flat circular peyote, and netting. The curved shape of the bead fits smoothly together in these stitches.

Delica beads, by Miyuki (and Toho Antiques, which are similar in size and appearance), are short cylinders with large holes relative to their size. They come in two sizes: small 1.5mm, about the same as a size 12 seed bead, and large, or 3.3mm, which is similar to a size 8 seed bead. There are more than 450 different colors of Delica. These beads are perfect for rectangular grid techniques such as loomwork, square stitch, peyote stitch, and brick stitch, where the beads fit tightly together in a stacking, block-like orientation.

Bead stores have an amazing variety of beads.

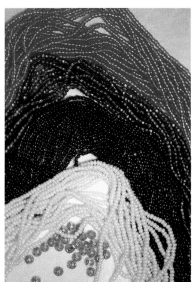

Seed beads.

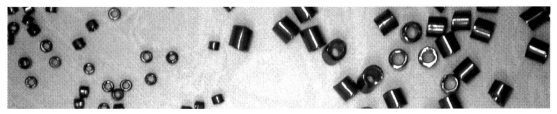

Delica beads.

Some other types of glass beads are:

Austrian Swarovski Crystals: Beads with a high lead content and precision faceting.

Bugle beads: Tube-shaped beads from 2mm to 30mm in length. These can be straight, hex cut, or twisted along their length.

Charlottes: These are seed beads that have been ground flat on one side.

Faceted beads: Seed beads ground with one or more flat surfaces. These include charlottes, three-cuts, and Austrian Swarovski Crystals.

Lampwork beads: Beads made one at a time by winding molten glass around a rod. The glass is heated using a small torch. In America, these beads are made as one-of-a-kind works of art. In Czechoslovakia, the same design of bead is made in larger quantities to sell, with apprentices spending much time learning to make beads exactly alike.

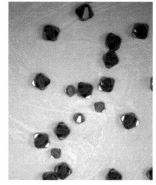

Left and above: Austrian Swarovski Crystals.

Bugle beads.

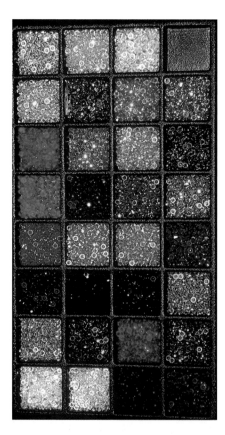

Charlottes.

Faceted beads.

Left and above: Lampwork beads.

Pressed glass: Beads pressed into a mold while the glass is soft. Common shapes are leaves, flowers, and drops, although many other shapes are available.

Three-cuts: Two-cut beads with random facets over their surface.

Two-cuts: Short bugle beads.

Any of the above beads can be made of different glass treatments such as:

Greasy: Semi-transparent beads.

Opaque: A solid-color bead commonly seen in traditional Native American beadwork.

Satin: Directional sheen due to tiny bubbles pulled through the glass as the bead is formed.

Transparent: Clear or colored glass that you can easily see through.

Pressed glass beads.

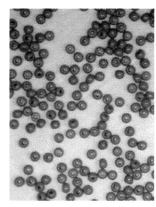

Pressed glass beads.

Three-cuts.

Two-cuts.

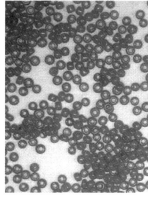

Greasy beads.

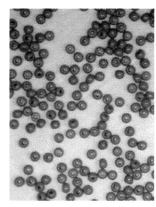

Opaque beads.

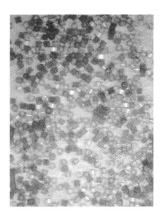

Satin beads.

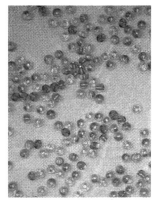

Transparent beads.

Where Did Those Beads Come From?

Today, most beads are made in Japan, Czechoslovakia, or France. You can't always tell where the beads you have came from without verifying it with your place of purchase, but here are a few things of common knowledge among beaders. If it's on a hank, it's from the Czech Republic. It is the only country that does this right now; however, if it's in a bag or a tube, it may have been removed from a hank and bagged, so it could be from any manufacturer. If it's a Delica or antique bead, it's definitely from Japan. Finally, beads from France have muted colors, which was common in the late eighteenth and early twentieth centuries. White hearts are also from France. Other than that, there are no common indicators for French beads.

Glass beads can also be made with a variety of finishes. Some finishes are durable, while others wear off easily. Finishes can fade in the sun, wear off from water, heat, abrasion, or oils in your skin. To test a bead for durability, let it sit in the sun for a week (in a clear bag in your car is a good place), sew a strand to some fabric and put it through the washer and dryer, or wear a strand of beads on your wrist for a week. If you find that the bead finish wears off, you may choose not to use it, or to use it in a project where it isn't exposed to your skin, if that's its downfall, or isn't exposed to direct sunlight, etc. Beads with delicate finishes are sometimes the most beautiful or the perfect ones for your project. That's when you have to decide how much handling your piece will have, and whether it will hold up over time. Sometimes it's better to change bead colors to make a lasting project, but other times you may just want to use the beads you've found. The following page has a list of some common seed bead finishes in alphabetical order, noting possible wear problems.

Photo by Myra Nunley

Semi-precious stone cabochons and fused glass make great centerpieces for beading. These brooches were designed and beaded by Corinne Loomer.

Color and Beads

When choosing bead colors, there are a few things to consider. The color you see in a bag or tube of beads is not always the same color that ends up in your beadwork. This is because of the many different types of glass used for beads and the finishes applied to them. Finishes like Aurora Borealis (AB) color each bead a little differently, so unless you use the beads together in a large area, you will only have a small part of the color group in the AB beads. Also, loose beads in a bag or tube show both the side of the bead and the hole. In most beadwork, only the side of the bead shows; hence if the bead hole has more color or a different color than the side of the bead, you will have a different shade of color in your beadwork than what appears in the bag or tube. Finally, beads of the same shade look different depending on whether they are made from transparent, opaque, satin, or another glass process. For these reasons, it is very important to make a test swatch of the colors you plan to use in projects with small areas of a variety or gradation of colors, such as the face in the Sun Catcher project or the Floral Tray (see pages 46 and 24, respectively). This way, you can be confident from the beginning of your project that you will have a finished piece which is worthy of all of your time and effort.

Aurora Borealis (AB), iridescent beads, or oil beads: A permanent finish that gives a rainbow-like sheen to the glass. They look very different individually in beadwork from the color you see in the tube. These are good beads to use in large spaces, but use them judiciously in a complex color scheme, or they can mottle the design.

Galvanized metallic beads: Very shiny, attractive beads with a thin metallic coating. This coating quickly wears away from abrasion and contact with skin. Do not use in bracelets or any high-wear project. Coat with clear fingernail polish to help retain the finish after your project is completed.

Lined: Transparent glass with a color painted inside. May fade in sunlight.

Luster: A transparent colored coating. This is sometimes called a Ceylon or pearl finish if the coating is white, giving the bead a pearlized look. Good durability.

Matte: A dull finish achieved by tumbling or etching. Good durability.

Silver-lined: A silver lining in the hole of the bead gives a bright, shiny appearance and durable color to transparent-colored beads. The silver can wear off over time.

Surface dyed beads: Used on all types, from opaque to silver-lined, for making popular colors such as purples and pinks. These colors may rub off or will fade over time.

Many of the above finishes are combined to make a different type of bead such as a matte AB finish, which is a matte bead with the iridescent effect of an AB coating.

Beads with an AB finish.

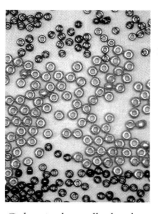

Galvanized metallic beads.

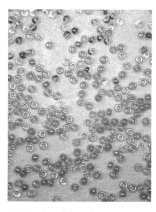

Color-lined beads.

Luster beads.

Matte-finished beads.

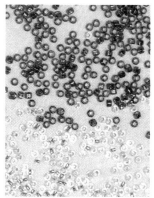

Silver-lined beads.

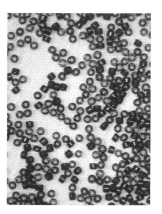

Beads with the color dyed onto the surface.

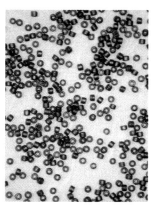

Matte beads with an AB finish.

These beads are in a category all their own!

Metal beads: Any bead made of metal.

Semi-precious stones: Beads of all shapes and sizes are made into semi-precious stone beads.

Steel cuts: Small metal beads, about a size 16, found in antique beaded bags. Some are round like seed beads, while some are faceted. Most are gold- or silver-toned. Some have a thin, metallic finish which is not very durable.

Triangles: Triangle beads are triangle-shaped as you look at them through the hole. In beadwork, the side showing is either one of the flat sides of the triangle, or one of the triangle edges, giving a distinct texture to the beadwork.

White hearts: A two-layer bead with a colored outer layer and a white inner glass layer. Originally, these beads were made to conserve on costly colored glass. Until recently, those available were all antique (they are being manufactured again).

Metal beads.

Semi-precious stone beads.

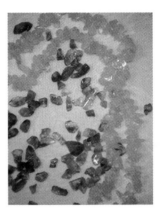
Semi-precious stone beads.

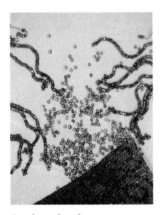
Steel cut beads.

Triangle beads.

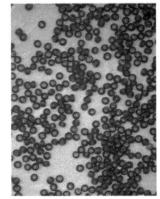
White heart beads.

Beading Terms

Here are a few general beading terms that appear throughout this book.

Beads can be packaged for sale in several ways. They are usually packaged by the bag or tube, by the hank or strand, or loose. Bags or tubes of beads are usually sold by weight, in grams and sometimes in ounces. A hank of beads is usually twelve 18- to 20-inch strands of beads with the ends tied together. Loose beads are usually large or specialty beads sold individually.

From left to right: loose beads, hanks of beads, and beads in bags and tubes.

Tools and Supplies

There is a variety of tools and supplies used in beading, with each beading technique having its own specific requirements and necessary tools and supplies. The following is an overview of the tools and supplies needed for the projects in this book.

Findings

Findings are metal parts used to put a piece of jewelry together, such as jump rings, clasps, earring posts, bead tips, and purse clasps. They are available in inexpensive base metals, as well as more expensive silver and gold. Taking time to choose a clasp or other finding that suits your project can greatly enhance the finished product. I recommend that you use quality findings that will not discolor, break, or cause skin allergies for the wearer. Be sure to ask for hypoallergenic findings when you purchase them if you have sensitive skin.

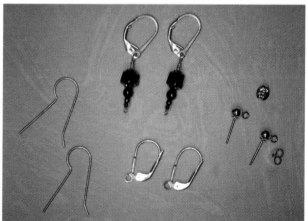

Above and right: A wide variety of findings.

Pliers

Pliers are used to shape wire and findings. There are four types commonly used with beadwork.

Needle nosed pliers are small pliers with pointed ends that look like a semi-circle from the end. They have small ridges on the inside face for a good grip. They are good all-purpose pliers for anything from bead knotting to just pulling a needle through a tough piece of suede.

Flat nosed pliers are like needle nosed pliers except that they do not have ridges and the nose end does not taper down to points. They are good for bending wire at right angles and gripping loops to wind wire around.

Round nosed pliers are thin, tapered pliers with small, round ends. They are used for winding wire into loops.

Chain nosed pliers are the same as needle nosed pliers except they are flat on the inside with no ridges. They are commonly used in wirework instead of needle nosed pliers, because they don't have ridges which would mar the wire.

Wire Cutters

Any wire cutter will do for beginning wirework, but as you become more adept, you will want better tools. The best wire cutters for jewelry close together parallel on one side, so you can make a clean cut through the wire, making a straight edge, rather than one tapered to a center ridge.

Wire

Wire comes in many colors, sizes, and metals. The sizes are determined by the gauge; the lower the number, the thicker the wire. Wire can be soft, hard, or somewhere in between. Soft wire is easily bent and hardens somewhat the more it is bent. Hard wire is more difficult to bend, so it is good for adding structure to a piece. Wires come in many shapes, including round, half round, square, triangle, and beaded. Square and triangle wire are often twisted to give added detail to a wirework piece.

Purse Frames

There is a variety of purse frames, both antique and contemporary, used for making beaded purses and bags. The majority has holes along the bottom of the frame to sew beadwork in place.

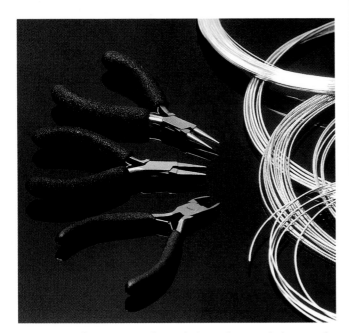

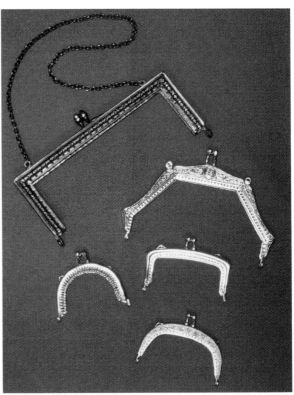

From top to bottom: round nosed pliers, flat nosed pliers, and wire cutters and beaded, round, and square sterling silver wire.

Antique and contemporary purse frames used in making beaded bags.

Needles

Any needle that can fit through your bead holes can be used for beading; however, thin needles, which easily slide through small bead holes, and long needles, which can pick up many beads at a time, are preferred. Here are several types of needles that make beading easier.

Beading needles are longer and thinner than sewing needles, so they fit through bead holes and allow you to pick up several beads at one time. Most beading needles have sharp ends. They range in size from the very thin size 16 to the thick size 10; these numbers correspond loosely to the bead size the needle will fit through.

Loomwork beading needles are 3 inches, or more, long, so that you can pass through a wide width of loomed beads.

Wire beading needles are a thin piece of wire, folded in half and twisted. The eye is the folded loop which collapses when pulled through a bead. Wire needles are used for threads which are too thick to thread in a standard beading needle, such as silk cord for knotted necklaces.

Bead embroidery needles are short like a cross stitch needle and have a blunt end, but are thin enough to accommodate size 11 beads.

Sharps needles are short, pointed needles with a small eye, used for appliqué and general hand stitching.

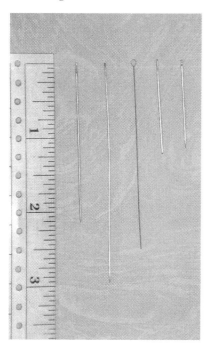

Left to right: Beading needle, loomwork needle, wire beading needle, bead embroidery needle, and sharps needle.

Threads and Cords

Beading thread can be any thread you can thread your needle with and get through a bead hole; however, glass beads get heavy as you add them to large projects. You should use the strongest thread you can find, which still gives you the drape you want. Some say that no thread can compare to the drape silk allows, but I have found that tension plays just as large a role in how a beaded fabric drapes.

About Thread Size Labeling Systems

Various systems have been used to designate thread thickness, resulting in a confusing set of numbers and letters to refer to the similar units of measurement.

Denier is an old French term for the weight in grams of 9000 meters of thread. Different fibers have different weights, so 40 denier nylon is not the same thickness as 40 denier silk. Denier is relevant only when used to compare the same fiber and it is only used for extruded fibers like silk and nylon and not spun fibers such as cotton or wool. For this reason, the European Union has banned the use of denier, and the new unit of measure is grams per kilometer of thread. The term denier still remains in use in the United States.

Common Thread Thickness Units

Nymo	Denier	Other threads that are the same thickness
OO	50	Silk size 50
O or A	60	Silamide twisted tailoring nylon
B		Silk size 380
D	1000	Upholstery Conso or Coats twisted nylon
E, F, FF		Gudebrod silk stringing twist with the same letter designations

Nymo

This is the most popular all-purpose beading thread currently available. Made of non-twisted bonded nylon filaments, Nymo comes in many colors and thicknesses. The number of filaments determines the thickness of the thread. Although Nymo has become the generic term for nylon beading thread, the brand name Nymo thread, by Belding Cortecelli, is generally the best quality. Nylon does not mildew or rot and makes a very durable thread for beadwork pieces.

Silk Cord

I like to use this thread for knitting, crochet, and beadweaving. It is very important to wax silk before beadweaving, or it will knot and kink. Silk is sized both by letters, as Nymo, and by denier, as shown in the table on the previous page. For knitting and crochet, 1000 denier is good and corresponds to about a size D Nymo.

Pearl Cotton

Sizes 12 and 8 are used for bead knitting, beaded knitting, and tubular crochet projects. This is a cotton thread and has its own numbering system. Size 12 is comparable to an E and size 8 is about as thick as F cord in silk. Pearl cotton tends to fray from the beads sliding on it, so it is not good for flat or round crochet or tatting where much of the cotton shows. If you wax the pearl cotton, it is a good thread for beadweaving with the larger size 8 and 6 beads.

Cebelia or Manuela

A tightly twisted cotton cord is better than pearl cotton for bead knitting, bead crochet, and tatting. The tight twist keeps the cord shiny and clean. There are many brand names available; however, they are not as readily available as pearl cotton. (For mail ordering, see the Supply Sources.)

Thread Conditioners

The traditional thread conditioner is beeswax. Slide the thread through the wax several times to apply an even, light coating. Then, slide the thread between your fingers several times to soften the wax and press it into the thread. If you use too much wax, the eye of the needle can close from wax build-up and even the bead holes can get filled with wax. To remove a wax plug from a needle, hold the needle between your thumb and forefinger to warm the wax in the eye. Also, it is better to use a thicker thread instead of heavily waxing a thinner one to give body to the bead fabric.

Pearl cotton.

There is a growing variety of tightly twisted cotton cords suitable for bead knitting, bead crochet, and tatting.

Nymo thread.

Silk cord.

Beeswax and Thread Heaven.

Thread Heaven is a newer, silicon-based thread conditioner that is lighter than beeswax and causes the end of the thread to be repelled from the working length. If you have lots of knotting problems involving the end of your thread, this can help you. Apply to the thread the same as beeswax. Use lightly and repeat if necessary.

Fray Check is an old sewing standby. It is useful for stiffening the end of the thread for easier threading into the eye of the needle. A light coating of glue will also work to create a stiff thread end that can function like a self-needle.

Basic Techniques

Beginning and Ending Threads

No matter how long a thread you use, eventually you have to end and restart your thread. For the best results, be sure to:
• Hide the threads invisibly in the work.
• Secure them in the work with a small knot or by weaving around in a circle so the thread cannot come out.
• Bury the new end in the beads so it does not show.

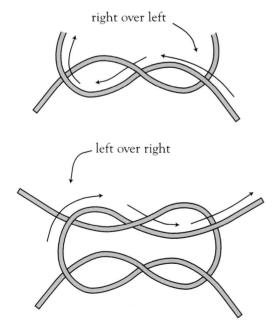

Figure 1-1

Stop Bead

A stop bead is used at the beginning of a project to prevent the beads from falling off the tail and provide tension for the first row of strung beads against which to weave.

To make a stop bead, pick up a bead and tie a square knot 6 inches from the tail, catching the bead in the knot. You will need to untie the bead later to weave in the tail thread. You can also wrap the tail around one of your fingers several times instead of using a stop bead.

Square Knot

The square knot (**Figure 1-1**) is my favorite knot in beadwork. Always remember: right over left, then left over right. This means cross the thread in your right hand over the thread in your left hand and around and through to tie a knot. Then, cross the thread that's now in your left hand over the thread in your right hand and around and through to tie a knot again. This makes a secure knot that won't slip out as easily as others. You may also want to put a small amount of clear nail polish on the knot to make sure it stays tied.

Overhand Knot

An overhand knot (**Figure 1-2**) is a good knot to use when weaving in threads. It catches the thread on itself, giving added protection against unraveling. To make an overhand knot, take a small stitch over a thread in the work and pull through until there is just a loop. Pass through the loop and pull tight. This knot is not as secure as the square knot but works well when used twice along with weaving the thread through several beads.

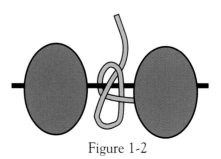

Figure 1-2

Weaving in Thread Ends

Weaving in thread ends means to pass the thread back through the beads, or fabric, knotting the thread and hiding it so that it is invisible.

For beadwork which is supported or will not get much handling, such as the Peyote Stitch Sun Catcher (on page 00), I just pass through adjacent beads several times.

For pieces that are handled often, such as the Herringbone Pinch Purse (on page 00), I tie an overhand knot, then pass through several beads in the stitch pattern and tie another overhand knot, then pass through several more beads and cut the thread close to the beadwork.

In knitted, crocheted, and tatted projects where there are non-beaded areas, make overhand knots in the non-beaded thread areas to secure the ends, then pass through the non-beaded area, encasing the thread in the stitches invisibly. Cut close to the needlework.

Bead Fabric

Large pieces of flat beadwork are sometimes referred to as bead fabric.

Breaking a Bead

Sometimes you will have a bead in the wrong place, and it is easier to break the bead rather than undo your work to correct the error. For example, when stringing beads for knitting, crocheting, or tatting, you may have added two blue beads and the pattern only calls for one, or, in netting, you find you've put six beads in a loop that's supposed to have five and you don't want to pull all of the beading out to get back to that point.

You can easily break a glass bead with flat nosed or needle nosed pliers, but if you do it the wrong way, you will cut your thread every time. You need to wrap the thread tightly around your index finger and carefully grab the bead (**Figure 1-3**). Turn your face away and squeeze the pliers until the bead breaks. You may also want to slide your hands between a folded towel so you can easily clean up the glass chips. Never break the bead by squeezing the pliers on the bead as shown in (**Figure 1-4**). This will cause the breaking bead to cut the thread.

This bead netted piece shows the fluid drape of the beading; this is why it is sometimes called "bead fabric."

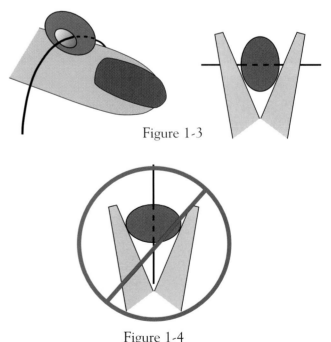

Figure 1-3

Figure 1-4

Sculptural beadwork is three-dimensional bead-work in any medium.

One Grecian Urn Perfume Nectar Necklace, designed and stitched by Delinda V. Amura. This sculptural vessel pendant is stitched in peyote with size 15 seed beads.

Antique loomed steel-cut purse made in France.

My Secret Garden, by Marlin Beads, is constructed with a combination of brick stitch and sculptural peyote stitch, using a variety of bead types.

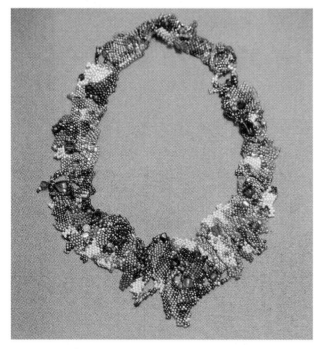

This neckpiece shows how changing bead sizes and random increases and decreases transforms peyote stitch. Collared Elegance in freeform peyote stitch, by Marlin Beads.

Beaded Vessel, designed and stitched by Sylvia Sur. Sculptural beadwork like this small container can be even more beautiful when viewed with back lighting.

Chapter 2
Loomwork

Beaded loomwork is a very old craft, used in the United States by Native Americans for generations. This technique of making a fabric of beads with thread is suitable for a large variety of items, from purses to belts and necklaces. There are many ways to add to the flat loomed piece, from adding fringe while the piece is on the loom to adding three-dimensional beading, giving depth to the finished piece.

Weaving beads on a loom is one of the quickest methods of beading, because a whole row of beads can be woven at one time. You give back some of the speed of weaving in setting up the loom in the beginning, and in hiding or decorating the warp threads at the end.

First, you start warping the loom, which means looping the warp thread back and forth across the loom, laying down equally spaced, parallel rows of thread. Next, you string the beads according to a design on a separate thread called the weft, and weave them between the warp threads. When you finish weaving the design, you cut the warp threads near the loom. Finally, you hide the cut ends of the warp ends at the back of the work or weave them up into the work.

There is a variety of looms available. The following sample is made on an inexpensive, small metal and wood loom sold in most craft stores. The following will show you how to warp the loom and create a sample.

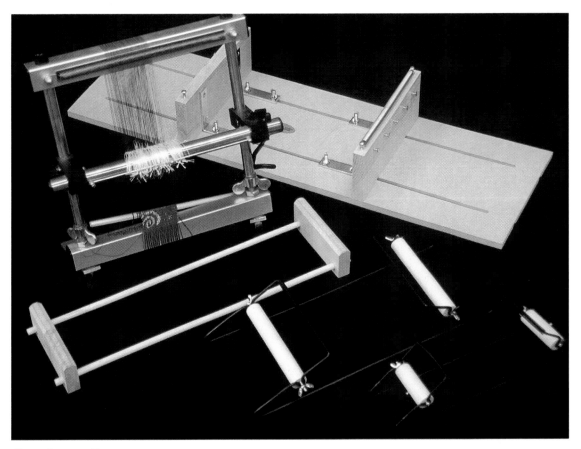

Several types of looms.

You Will Need

Delica beads, in the colors shown in
the Loomwork Sample design chart
Size D Nymo

Size 10 beading needle
Beading loom
Glue

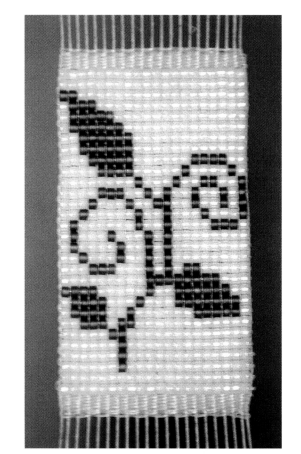

To warp the loom:

1. Roll the loom's dowels so the screws are facing away from the loom. Tighten the wing nuts.

2. Pull the thread from the spool, but do not cut it. Tie a square knot around the screw on one of the dowels.

3. Guide the thread up over the springs, around the screw on the other dowel (**Figure 2-1**).

4. Guide the thread back over the springs again so that it rests in the next slot between the springs (**Figure 2-2**). Continue looping the thread back and forth, over the springs and around the screws until there are 21 threads across the loom, each in its own slot. Keep the tension even.

5. Tie the thread to the screw and cut the thread from the spool. These are your warp threads. You always use one more warp thread than the number of beads in the width of the bead design chart.

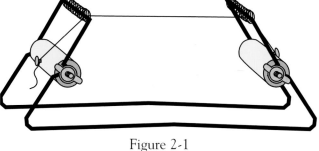

Figure 2-1

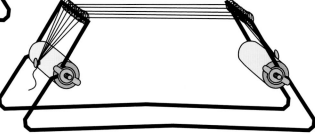

Figure 2-2

To begin weaving:

1. Tie an 8-foot length of thread to the bottom leftmost warp thread, leaving a 12-inch tail to weave in later. Thread the needle.

2. Pass the needle under the warp threads to the right. Read the Loomwork Sample design chart from the bottom to the top, left to right. Pick up beads for Row 1 (all cream beads), and push them up against the warp threads so that each bead sits between two warp threads.

3. Pass the needle back through the beads, holding the beads against the warp with your index finger so the needle passes above the warp threads, locking the beads in place.

4. Repeat Steps 2 and 3 for each row of the design chart.

To make a thread selvage:

1. Weave in and out of the warp threads without beads for about 1/4 inch (**Figure 2-3**).

2. Put a dab of glue along the last two or three rows of thread weaving. Let dry.

3. Thread the 12-inch tail at the beginning of the weaving and repeat Steps 1 and 2.

4. Cut the beadwork from the loom 1/8 inch beyond the thread selvages.

5. Fold the woven thread selvages under. Glue them to the beads in place with a small amount of glue.

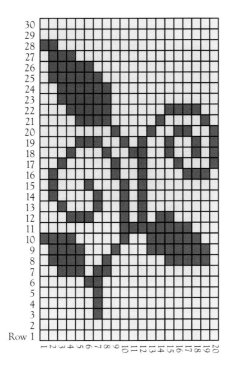

■ #859
□ #157

Loomwork Sample
design chart

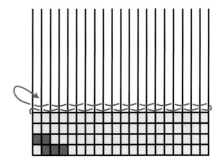

Figure 2-3

Here's how the small loom looks after you've bent the ends up. They are almost perpendicular to the table so you can weave a larger piece without winding the beading.

Beaded Loomwork Floral Tray

You Will Need

Sudberry House Petite Serving Tray #6565
Delica beads, as shown in the Color Key
   for Floral Loomwork Tray
1 large spool size D Nymo

1 small spool size B Nymo
Size 10 or 12 loom beading needle
Loom
Glue

The idea for a beadwork tray came from the beautiful antique beaded needlepoint tray on page 107. I chose some of my favorite flowers for the design and made the graph from my watercolor painting. Then, I took the pattern from the loom-work sample and repeated it randomly in white and mint to add texture to an otherwise plain background.

Unless you own a loom that is wide enough for 177 warp threads, you will need to make this piece in sections, as I did. I have written the instructions so you can make this piece in strips on a small loom. If you use a larger loom, you will need to adjust the number of warp threads to the most you can fit for each section.

Finished size: 7 by 10 inches (beadwork area only)

I learned a trick from Delinda Vannebrightyn Amura, a national teacher and author of The Illuminated Beading Manuscripts Book II The Loom, *to make the loom big enough to bead a larger area without having to wind the growing beadwork onto the dowels. To fit the 7-inch height of beading onto your small loom, before beginning, pull the ends so they are almost perpendicular to the bottom wire. Adjust the loom so that all of the corners lie flat on the table.*

1. Warp the loom as described for the sample of loomwork on page 22 using size D Nymo, until you have filled it with warp threads. Use size B Nymo for the last warp thread so the seams will not show on the finished piece.

2. Count how many warp threads you have and then subtract 1. This is the number of beads you will be weaving for this section of the tray. Use sticky notes on the Beaded Loomwork Floral Tray design chart to isolate the section you will be weaving.

3. Beginning in the bottom left corner, weave the section of the pattern you have isolated. Make thread woven selvages as described for the sample on page 23. Cut from the loom.

4. Repeat Steps 1 to 3 for the next sections of the design, each time moving the sticky notes to show only the part of the design you are weaving.

5. When all of the sections are completed, stitch them together by weaving through three or four beads in each row along the adjoining selvages (**Figure 2-4**).

6. Place the finished beadwork into the tray following the manufacturer's instructions.

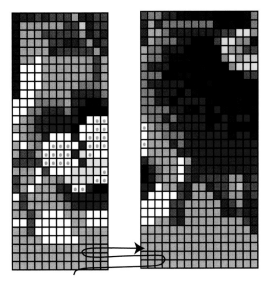

Figure 2-4

Color Key for Floral Loomwork Tray

- ▣ Background #829, 50 grams
- ☐ Background #211, 9 grams
- ▢ Pansy leaves #372, less than 1 gram
- ▤ Pansy leaves #724, less than 1 gram
- ■ All leaves #663, 3 grams
- ▢ Violet leaves #374, less than 1 gram
- ▨ Violet leaves #373, 2 grams
- ▦ Violet leaves #859, 3 grams
- ■ Violet and Pansy leaves #275, 3 grams
- ☐ Sweet Pea leaves #733, less than 1 gram
- ☐ Sweet Pea leaves #877, 3 grams
- ▨ Sweet Pea leaves #372, less than 1 gram
- ▦ Sweet Pea leaves #380, less than 1 gram
- ▦ Sweet Pea leaves #724, 3 grams
- ☐ Flower centers #160, less than 1 gram
- ▢ Johnny Jump-up #053, less than 1 gram

- ☐ Sweet Pea #234, less than 1 gram
- ▨ Sweet Pea #245, less than 1 gram
- ▨ Sweet Pea #855, less than 1 gram
- ▦ Sweet Pea #1371, less than 1 gram
- ▦ Sweet Pea # 362 , less than 1 gram
- ▨ Red Pansy #295, less than 1 gram
- ■ Red Pansy #296, 2 grams
- ▨ All Flowers # 80 , 2 grams
- ▨ All Flowers #881 , 2 grams
- ▦ All Flowers #661, 2 grams
- ▨ All Flowers # 216, 2 grams
- ▢ Pansies #880, 2 grams
- ▦ All Flowers #1379, 1 gram
- ■ Pansies #464, 2 grams
- ■ Pansies #278, 1 gram
- ■ Pansies #310, less than 1 gram

Beaded Loomwork Floral Tray design chart

Chapter 3
Square Stitch

quare stitch is visually very close to loom-work, because the beads are aligned in the same straight rectilinear grid pattern of rows and columns.

In square stitch, the beads are added to the beginning row of beads one bead at a time. You put on a bead, then loop through the bead below on the first row, then come back up through the new bead. You add each bead this way to the end of the row, then repeat the process starting on the opposite side.

Because you follow the pattern back and forth in a zigzag, you have to pay attention to the direction of the work with non-symmetrical designs.

Square stitch creates a very elastic fabric, with a great deal of drape. The first row is awkward, and you'll need to keep the beads in place as you stitch. Once you complete about three rows, it is easier.

Square Stitch Sample

You Will Need

Delica beads, in the colors shown in the Square Stitch Sample design chart	Size B or D Nymo
	Size 10 beading needle

Finished size: 1-1/8 inches by 2-1/8 inches

1. Thread the needle with a 4-foot length of thread and add a stop bead.

2. String 18 cream-colored Delicas; this is the first row of the Square Stitch Sample design chart, from bead 1 to bead 18.

3. String one cream-colored bead. This is bead number 18 in the second row of the design chart.

4. Pass through the 18th bead from the first row (**Figure 3-1**).

5. Pass through the 18th bead from the second row (**Figure 3-2**). The first row is very flexible. Pull each stitched bead tight, holding the beads in place so they stay parallel to the same number bead in the previous row. Use the stop bead to keep the beads in the first row snug.

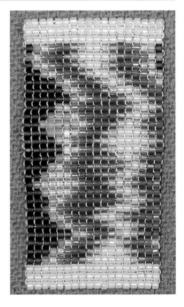

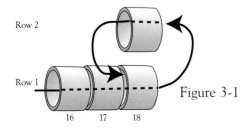

Figure 3-1

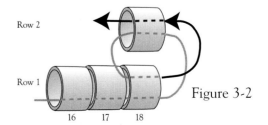

Figure 3-2

6. String the 17th bead in Row 2 on the design chart.

7. Pass through the 17th bead from the first row (**Figure 3-3**).

8. Pass through the 17th bead from the second row (**Figure 3-4**).

9. Continue adding beads, looping through the adjacent bead in the previous row, then back through the new bead until the end of the row.

Repeat in the opposite direction, adding beads 1 through 18 of Row 3. Continue in this manner for each row.

10. When you've finished the pattern, weave in the working thread and cut close to the beading.

11. Untie the stop bead and remove it from the thread. Thread the needle with the 12-inch tail and loop through the first row (**Figure 3-5**). This evens out the tension in the first row so it has the same elasticity as the rest of the piece. Weave in this thread and cut close to the beading.

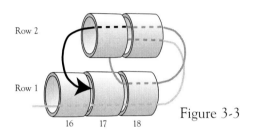

Figure 3-3

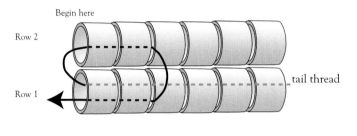

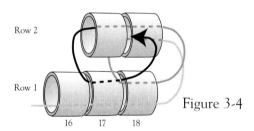

Figure 3-4

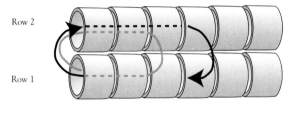

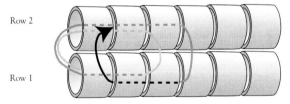

Figure 3-5

□ #157	■ #862
■ #859	■ #792
□ #829	■ #857
▨ #078	▢ #072
■ #166	

Square Stitch Sample design chart

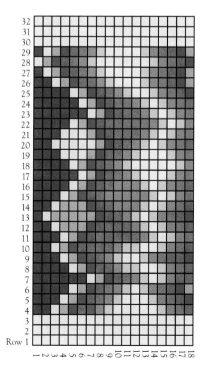

Square Stitch Table Setting

You Will Need

Wooden salt and pepper shakers, milk can style, 3-3/16 inches high by 1-3/4-inch diameter

Wooden napkin ring, colonial style, 1-1/4 inches tall by 1-3/4 inches wide

Size 8 seed beads

    16 grams or 3/4 oz. of green

6 grams or 1/4 oz. of pink

6 yellow

77 grams or 2-3/4 oz. white

Size D white Nymo

Size 10 beading needle

White craft paint and brush or enamel spray paint

This table setting is quick to make in size 8 seed beads. The beaded covers for the salt and pepper shakers are beaded flat, then attached around the middle of the wooden shakers. The napkin ring is worked in the round on a wooden base. The coaster is a flat piece of beadwork which can be stitched to a padded fabric base or used alone.

Finished sizes:

Coaster: 3-3/4 inches square

Salt and pepper shakers: 1-1/4-inch high beaded area on 3-3/16-inch high by 1-3/4-inch diameter shakers

Napkin ring: 3/4-inch wide beaded area on a 1-3/4-inch diameter wooden napkin ring

Paint

1. Paint the wooden salt and pepper shakers and napkin ring with white paint. Let dry.

To make the coaster:

1. Thread the needle with a 8-foot length of Nymo. Tie a stop bead 18 inches from the tail.

2. String Row 1 of the Coaster design chart.

3. Bead the coaster following the pattern. Weave in the end and cut close to the beading.

4. Thread the 18-inch tail and loop through the first and second rows as described for the Square Stitch Sample (on page 28) to even out the tension of the first row. Weave in the tail and cut close to the beading.

5. If desired, cut a piece of felt 1/8 inch smaller than the finished coaster and stitch along the edges to the beads.

Note: The coaster is shown on its side.

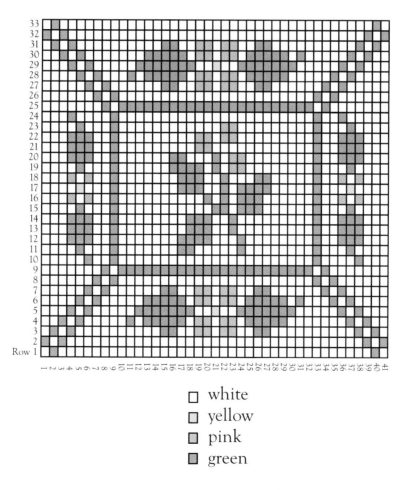

☐ white
☐ yellow
☐ pink
☐ green

Coaster design chart

To make the salt and pepper shakers:

1. Thread the needle with a 8-foot length of Nymo. Tie a stop bead 12 inches from the tail.

2. String Row 1 of the Salt and Pepper Shaker design chart.

3. Bead the design following the pattern.

4. Stretch the beadwork around one shaker and stitch through the adjacent beads of the first and last rows to close the beadwork around the shaker (**Figure 3-6**).

5. Weave in the tail and working thread and cut close to the beadwork.

6. Repeat Steps 1 to 5 for the pepper shaker, using the "P" in place of the "S."

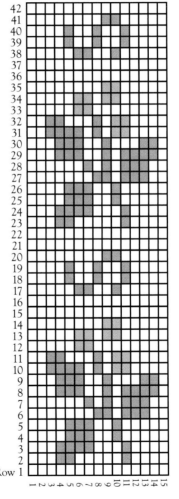

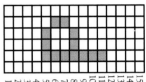

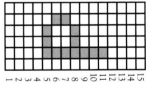

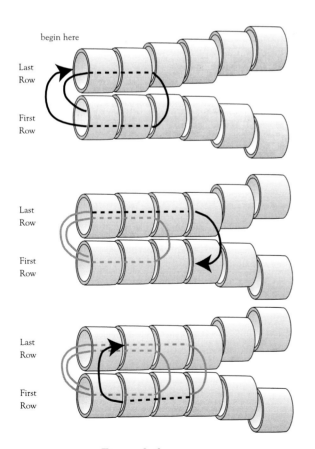

Figure 3-6

□ white
□ yellow
▨ pink
▧ green

Salt and Pepper Shaker
design chart

To make the napkin ring:

1. Thread the needle with a 8-foot length of Nymo. String 65 white beads and pass through them again to form a circle (**Figure 3-7**).

2. Tighten the circle of beads over the indentation on one end of the wooden base. Tie the tail and working thread into a square knot, leaving a 6-inch tail to weave in later. This is the first row of the design. The visible gaps between the beads will be evened out as you bead the next rows.

3. Bead Row 2 of the Napkin Ring design chart. The first and last row will be tight in the groove of the napkin ring. All of the other rows will be loose and elastic.

4. When you finish the round, pass through the first and last beads of the first two rows to attach the first and last beads of Row 2 together (**Figure 3-8**). Repeat this for each row.

5. Stitch Row 3 in the opposite direction around the napkin ring.

6. Continue stitching around, alternating the starting direction of the stitching with each row until you finish the beadwork. Pass through the last row of beads again and pull tightly, so the last row fits into the indentation on the napkin ring. Knot the thread. Weave in the ends.

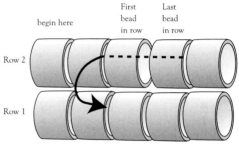

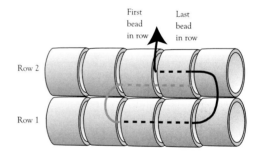

Figure 3-8

□ white
□ yellow
▨ pink
▨ green

Napkin Ring
design chart

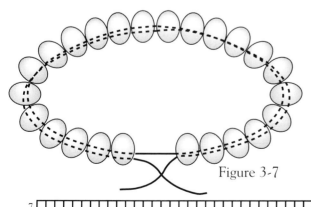

Figure 3-7

Rows labeled 7, 6, 5, 4, 3, 2, Row 1. Columns numbered 1 through 66.

Chapter 4

Brick and Ladder Stitch

Brick stitch is well named, because the beads are arranged like a brick wall, with each row offset by half a bead width. The bead holes sit vertically, and each bead is added by attaching it to the loop between two beads in the previous row.

Ladder stitch is the most common way to begin the brick stitch, because it provides a row of beads with loops of thread between the vertical bead holes, ready for brick stitch. Brick stitch is sometimes called Comanche or Cheyenne stitch due to its usage by Native American tribes of the same names.

Brick stitch box in progress.

Brick Stitch and Ladder Stitch Sample

You Will Need

Delica beads, in the colors shown in the Brick Stitch Sample design chart

Size B or D Nymo
Size 10 beading needle

Finished size: 1-1/8 by 2-1/4 inches

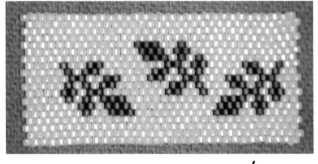

To make the first row in ladder stitch:

1. Thread the needle with a 6-foot length of thread. Tie a stop bead 6 inches from the tail and pick up 32 cream-colored beads. This is Row 1 on the Brick Stitch Sample design chart.

2. Hold the beads in your left hand (**Figure 4-1**) and pass through the second bead from the needle, toward the needle. Pull tight so the bead closest to the needle and the bead you passed through tighten together about 6 inches from the stop bead (**Figure 4-2**).

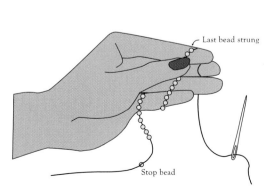

Last bead strung

Stop bead

Figure 4-1

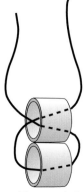

Figure 4-2

3. Pass the needle through the next bead away from the needle, toward the two beads just stitched, and pull the thread through, letting the three beads hang just before you pull them tight so they can twist into place on the growing ladder of beads (**Figure 4-3**).

4. Repeat Step 3 until all 32 beads are stitched together. Pass back through the second to last bead. Untie and remove the stop bead and tie the tail and working thread into a square knot (**Figure 4-4**). This is Row 1 of the Brick Stitch Sample design chart stitched into ladder stitch.

To make the sample in brick stitch:

1. Continuing with the ladder-stitched beads, pick up bead 1 and bead 2 in Row 2 on the design chart.

2. Pass through the thread between the last two beads on the ladder stitch piece (**Figure 4-5**).

3. Pass down through bead 2 on Row 2 (**Figure 4-6**). Pull tight.

4. Pick up the next bead in the row. Pass through the next loop between the next two beads in the previous row. Pass down through the bead just strung.

5. Repeat Step 4 across the row.

6. Continue each row the same as Steps 1 through 5, working back and forth across each row of the design chart. Weave in the ends.

Figure 4-3

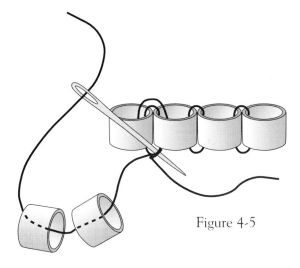

Figure 4-5

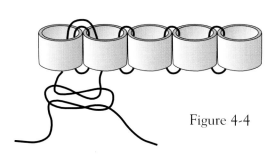

Figure 4-4

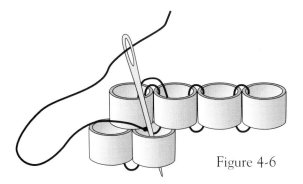

Figure 4-6

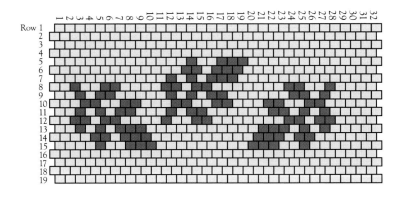

■ #859

□ #157

Brick Stitch Sample
design chart

Ladybug Box

This box is special to me, because it is the first project I ever taught. It was a big step for me because I am much more comfortable alone in a room with my needlework than standing in front of a class. I'll always remember those polite students, who really knew more about beading than I did at the time.

This is a fun box to make, although the first three rows are a bit of a struggle. It is important to pay close attention to the increases, so that the pattern lines up properly from the beginning, so you can stitch the rest of the box trouble-free.

Finished size: 2 inches wide by 1-1/2 inches high (beaded area is 1-1/4 inches high)

To paint the wooden box:

1. Paint the area you will bead over in white.

2. Paint the rims, bottom, and lid in black. Let dry.

3. Spray with a clear gloss finish. Let dry.

How to read the Ladybug Box design chart:

1. Each colored rectangle is one bead. The color matches the bead color to use.

2. White rectangles with diagonal lines indicate where you increase or decrease your bead count to shape the beaded cover so it fits snugly around the curved box.

3. You start at the upper left corner and work left to right and down.

How to increase:
Increase beads have arrows pointing to the left. When you get to one of these beads in the chart, put on one bead and pass the needle through the same thread loop as the bead before. You have two beads in the same thread loop (**Figure 4-7**).

How to decrease:
Decrease beads have arrows pointing to the right. When you get to one of these beads in the chart, put on one bead and skip the next thread loop. Pass through the second thread loop over. You decreased by one bead (**Figure 4-8**).

To work Row 1:
1. Thread the needle with a 6-foot length of thread. Start 2 feet in from the end and make a tight ladder stitch 82 beads long using the light blue beads. You will use up some of the tail in making the ladder, and the rest will be for weaving in once you have stitched about three rows on the box.

2. Make sure your ladder is not twisted (straighten out any twists). Join into a circle by passing through the first bead (**Figure 4-9**).

3. Put the loop of ladder stitch in the indentation below the box's top rim. Tie a square knot with the tail and working thread.

To work Row 2:
1. Pick up two light blue beads and start to brick stitch around the box, following the color placement in the design chart.

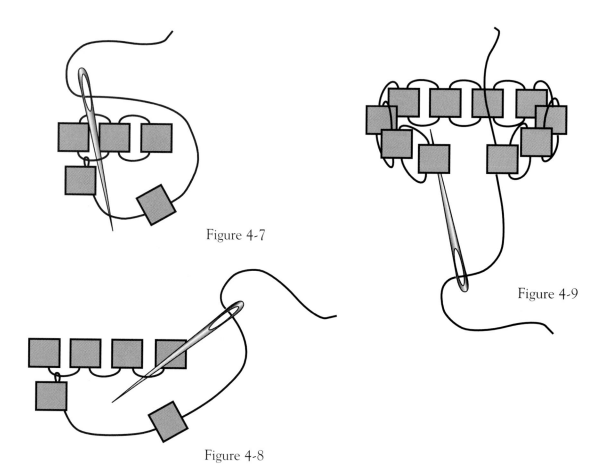

Figure 4-7

Figure 4-9

Figure 4-8

2. At the end of the row, pass through the first bead in the row (**Figure 4-10**), then back through the last bead in the row to close the round (**Figure 4-11**).

To work Row 3:

1. Pick up two beads. Pass through the thread loop between the first and second beads in Row 2. Pass through the second bead and continue around the box, following the chart.

2. Increase where the arrows indicate by stitching the bead marked with an arrow in the same space as the stitch before it.

3. Close the round by passing up through the first bead in this row and one bead in Row 2 (**Figure 4-12**).

4. Pass down through one bead in Row 2 and the first bead in Row 3 (**Figure 4-13**).

To work Row 4:

1. Pick up two beads. Pass through the thread loop between the second and third bead in Row 3.

2. Continue around, finishing as you did Row 3.

To finish the box:

Work brick stitch around the box. On odd rows, stitch between the first and second beads of the previous row. On even rows, stitch between the second and third beads of the previous row. Watch how the beginning beads line up to make sure that you are starting your rows correctly.

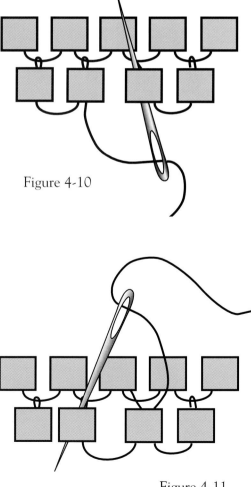

Figure 4-10

Figure 4-11

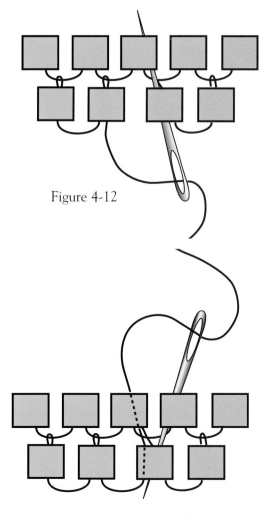

Figure 4-12

Figure 4-13

Ladybug Box
design chart

□ #879
■ #683
■ Black
□ #107
■ #916
■ #656
■ #797
■ #275

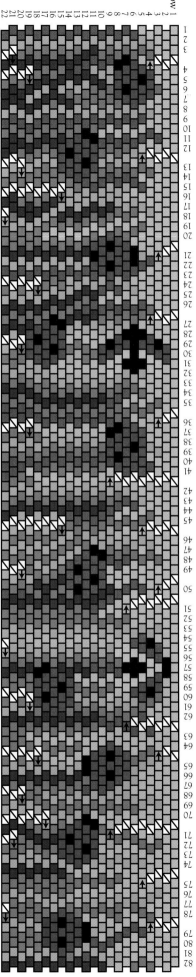

Chapter 5
Peyote Stitch

The stitch commonly known as peyote in North America is the basis for all netting stitches, and versions of it exist from beading samples from the Middle East dating back 2,000 years. The name peyote comes from a version of this stitch that is used by Native Americans to make religious items such as rattles and fan handles for peyote-based ceremonies. The Native American version of peyote (which is also known as gourd stitch when used for non-religious items) is different from the popular symmetrical version. For a comprehensive discussion of that technique, refer to *Native American Beadwork*, by Georg Barth (see the Bibliography).

The popular version of peyote has become the stitch of choice for many beaders because it is quick, easy, and versatile when compared to most other beading stitches. There are three main variations to the single bead version of this stitch:

• **Flat peyote:** Odd or even count. These are the versions you will learn in this book.
• **Tubular peyote:** Odd or even count.
• **Circular flat peyote:** You will learn this version in Chapter 6, Bead Netting.

Other variations use two or three beads instead of one; these are known as two-drop and three-drop peyote. These are faster and easier to work than the one-drop version. The only difference from standard peyote stitch is that two or three beads are picked up instead of one for each stitch.

Because the grid for this stitch is not based on a square, and you put on every other bead to make a row, reading peyote stitch charts takes some getting used to. I like to use a sticky note to cover all of the rows except the ones I've completed and the one I am working on, so I can easily find my place.

In working a flat piece of peyote with an odd bead count, at the end of odd numbered rows, your needle is not coming out of the correct bead to put the next bead on. So, you have to learn to make a figure-eight turn at the end of odd rows of flat peyote pieces to position your needle for the next bead.

In tubular even peyote, you have to learn to recognize the first bead you put on at the beginning of a row because you need to step up through it to start the next row. "Step up" means going through the last bead of the previous row, then up through the first bead of the row you are finishing. This shifts each new row over by one bead. Charts for circular peyote stitch are sometimes marked with a diagonal line indicating the first bead in each row.

Tubular odd peyote does not have turns so you do not have to position your needle at the end of rows, nor do you have a step up; you keep spiraling around.

Idele Gilbert is adept at miniatures stitched using peyote stitch and Delica beads, like these fish swimming in a pearl stream.

Photo by Myra Nunley

Amulet bags, such as this peyote-stitched example designed and beaded by Carole Tripp in 1997, helped the current popularity of beading. Beading has steadily grown in popularity since the late 1980s when magazine articles such as Alice Korach's bead knitting and Virginia Blakelock's fabulous loomwork neckpieces were published. When Alice founded Bead & Button Magazine in 1994, she established beading as a craft form.

Prairie Dawn, by Shonna Neuhart, in peyote stitch.

Sculptural peyote stitch around a ceramic molded face, designed and beaded by Carole Tripp.

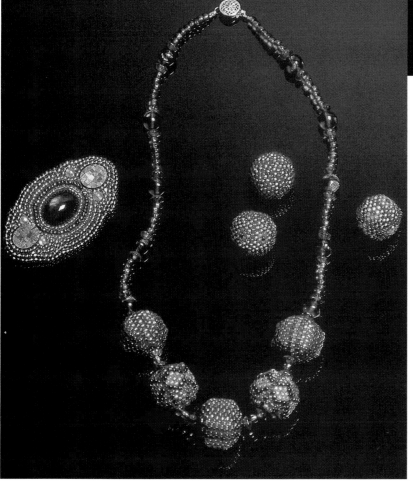

Peyote-stitched beads strung into a necklace and loose beads are shown with a brooch made of beads stitched around a cabochon. Designed and beaded by Sylvia Sur.

Peyote Stitch 43

Peyote stitch figure, by Marlin Beads.

This little circus monkey is made in two-drop peyote, where two beads are picked up for each stitch. Circus Monkey was designed and beaded by Elizabeth Gourley.

You Will Need

Delica beads, in the colors shown in the
Peyote Stitch Sample design chart

Size B or D Nymo
Size 10 beading needle

Finished size: 1-1/8 inches by 2-1/8 inches

1. Thread the needle with a 6-foot length of
thread. Tie a stop bead 6 inches from the tail and
pick up 39 cream-colored beads. This is Row 1
and Row 2 on the Peyote Stitch Sample design
chart.

2. Pick up bead 39 in Row 3 and pass through the
third bead from the needle (bead 38 in Row 2)
(**Figure 5-1**). Pull tight.

3. Pick up the next bead in Row 3, skip the next
bead on the thread, and pass through the following bead on the thread (bead 36 in Row 2)
(**Figure 5-2**). Pull tight.

4. Repeat Step 3 across the row, picking up a bead
from the chart, skipping a bead on the thread, and
passing through the next bead on the thread.

5. Pick up the last bead. Follow the thread path
in **Figure 5-3** to add the last bead in Row 3 and
position the needle to begin Row 4. You make this
turn at the end of every odd-numbered row.

6. Continue following the design, working peyote
stitch back and forth.

7. Weave in the ends.

begin here

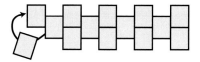

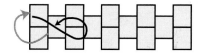

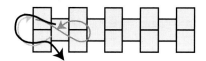

Figure 5-3

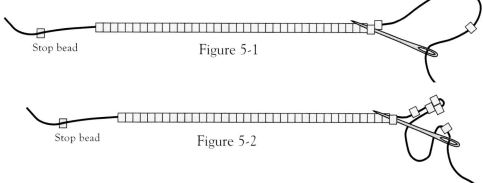

Stop bead   Figure 5-1

Stop bead   Figure 5-2

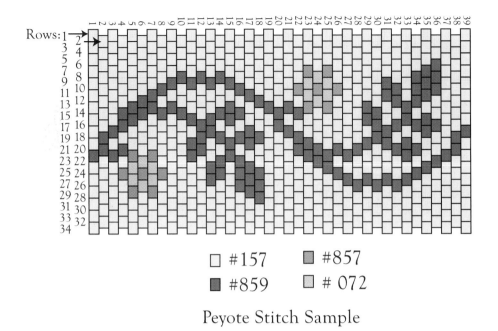

Rows:

□ #157   ■ #857
■ #859   ■ # 072

Peyote Stitch Sample
design chart

Peyote Stitch Beaded Sun Catcher

You Will Need

Floating glass picture frame, at least 5 by 7 inches with a landscape orientation and enough space between the two pieces of glass to fit the width of the beads (check this by actually putting a bead between the two pieces of glass)

Delica beads, in the colors shown in the Sun Catcher design chart
Delica beads in two contrasting colors (light and dark) for a starter strip
Size B or D white Nymo
Size 10 beading needle

This project uses a floating glass picture frame in a whimsical wire stand to display the peyote stitch panel, rather than a traditional sun catcher which hangs in a window. The transparent and opaque beads contrast as sunlight glistens through the beadwork, and white beading thread keeps the true color of the beads.

You will start this project by making a reusable starter strip of peyote stitch. This is a wonderful tool for starting peyote stitch projects without struggling with the first three rows and the uneven beginning tension common to peyote work. You

first bead a false row onto this foundation and then remove it after you finish several rows of the project. This separates the reusable starter strip from the project. The process creates a smooth beginning to the beadwork, so the tension is uniform throughout. The starter strip is well worth the time and effort because it can be used again for starting other flat peyote stitch projects.

Finished size: 5-1/2 inches wide by 5 inches tall in a 5- by 7-inch horizontal frame

The colors in this piece change when the light shines through the beads, illuminating the translucent beads.

To make the starter strip:

1. Thread the needle with an 8-foot length of thread and tie a stop bead 6 inches from the tail. String 120 Delica beads, consisting of 24 repeats of four light beads and one dark bead.

2. Work five rows of flat peyote, making a vertical stripe with the dark beads so you have a five-bead repeat. This helps, because now you can easily count by fives when you add your project beads. There will be 60 beads in each of the two rows.

3. Weave in the ends and cut close to the beadwork.

To make the sun catcher:

1. Thread the needle with a 6-foot length of thread. Loosely anchor the thread in the starter strip. Bead one row of 56 beads to the starter strip. This is your temporary row and can be a contrasting color. You will remove this row after you bead three or four more rows. Be very careful not to split the thread in the starter strip with the needle while beading this row and the next.

2. Bead the first three to five rows of the pattern from the Sun Catcher design chart.

3. Separate the starter strip from the project by unthreading the beads from Step 1. Once you begin to separate the row, it pulls apart easily.

4. Remove all of the beads on the thread from the first temporary row and weave the thread into the sun catcher. Cut close to the beading.

5. Continue beading the pattern in peyote stitch until complete. Weave in the thread ends among the opaque beads so the threads will not show through the transparent beads in the sunlight.

6. Insert the finished beadwork into the picture frame and place on a counter or window sill, or in a window box, so the sunlight filters through the beads.

Sun Catcher
design chart

Chapter 6

Netting

Making a net with beads is just a matter of adding more beads to peyote stitch; the basic structure of both techniques is the same. Netting usually has an odd number of beads in loops, and each loop is attached by passing through the center bead in a loop on the previous row. Similar to peyote, odd count and even count flat netting have different turns at the ends of rows, and round netting has the shifting first stitch, as in tubular peyote.

A flat bead netted piece can be described by the number of beads in each stitch, such as three-bead netting, which is when you pick up three beads for every stitch. You can increase the width of the work by adding more beads in each stitch, such as progressing from three-bead netting to five-bead netting to seven-bead netting. Lowering the number of beads in each stitch decreases the width of the fabric. This makes it is easy to shape netting around curved jars and balls.

Because netting is made of loops of beads, it is a very loose stitch, which is dramatically affected

Detail of a skirt from Bali. The bead-netted pattern is made using tiny size 16 seed beads.

by anything placed beneath it because of the space between the stitches. When stitching a pattern in netting and using a lining, use a background fabric which blends with the background beads in the pattern.

Bead Netting Sample

— *You Will Need* —

Size 11 seed beads, in the colors shown in the Bead Netting Sample design chart	Size B Nymo
	Size 11 or 12 beading needle

Finished size: 1-1/8 inches by 2-1/8 inch

1. Thread the needle with a 6-foot length of thread. Tie a stop bead 6 inches from the tail.

2. String 21 beads. This is Row 1 on the Bead Netting Sample design chart.

3. String three beads and pass through the eighth bead away from the needle, including the three

beads just strung, toward the tail end of the thread (**Figure 6-1**).

Figure 6-1

4. String three additional beads and pass the needle through the fourth bead away from the last stitch (**Figure 6-2**).

5. Repeat Step 4 across the row.

6. Tighten the beads together across the row, then pick up five beads and pass through the center bead in the last three-bead loop, going in the opposite direction (**Figure 6-3**) to make the turn around to the next row.

7. Repeat Step 4 across the row. After the last three-bead loop is added, repeat Step 6 to make the turn around to the next row.

8. Continue as in Step 7, following the color pattern in the design chart below. Weave in the ends.

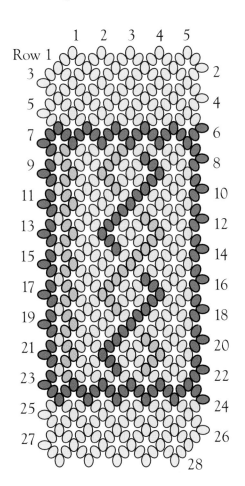

Bead Netting Sample
design chart

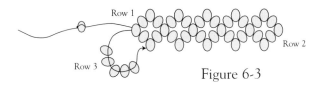

Figure 6-2

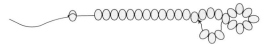

Figure 6-3

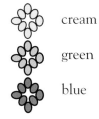

cream

green

blue

Bead Netted Knot Design

Many ethnic beadwork pieces, such as the detail of the skirt from Bali on page 49, use rich patterns in bead netting. Here is a flat beaded knot pattern using the same technique for a trivet, coaster, or wall decoration. Bead netting easily lends itself to Celtic knot patterns because of the strong diagonal lines in its construction.

Finished size: 5-1/2 inches square

1. Thread the needle with an 8-foot length of thread. Tie a stop bead 6 inches from the tail and string 113 dark beads. This is Row 1 on the Netted Knot design chart.

2. Follow Steps 3 through 6 of the Bead Netting Sample (on pages 49 and 50), then continue as in Step 7, following the color pattern in the design chart. Weave in the ends.

3. Place the beadwork in the picture frame to use as a coaster, trivet, or hang on the wall.

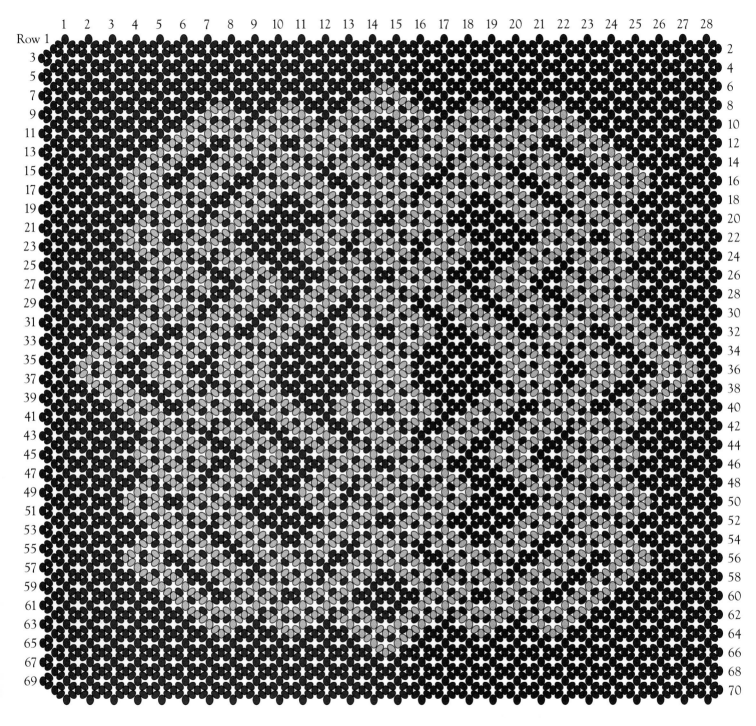

| | | | | | | | | | | | | | | | | | | | | | | | | | | | |
|1|2|3|4|5|6|7|8|9|10|11|12|13|14|15|16|17|18|19|20|21|22|23|24|25|26|27|28|

Row 1

light beads

dark beads

Netted Knot
design chart

Bead Netting Christmas Ornament

This project truly shows the connection between peyote stitch and bead netting. The ornament is stitched in the round, beginning with flat circular peyote stitch and progressing to netting. The snowflake pattern is made by repeating a specific color sequence six times around the piece. Finally, thin wire is strung through the center bead of each three-bead loop on the last row to keep the piece flat. You can make this pattern in any size seed beads to change the piece's finished size. You can also make earrings by only stitching the first 10 rounds in size 15 beads. Use the thickest wire which will fit through the beads to form the finished piece into shape.

Finished size: 2-1/8 inches in diameter

1. Thread the needle with an 8-foot length of thread. String three blue beads and tie into a circle with a square knot. Row 1 (a circle) is now completed on the Bead Netted Ornament design chart. Pass through the first bead to prepare for Row 2 (**Figure 6-4**).

2. Pick up two blue beads and pass through the next bead on Row 1 (**Figure 6-5**). Repeat twice. Pass through the first bead in the row to prepare for Row 3 (**Figure 6-6**).

Figure 6-4

Figure 6-5

Darker beads show current stitch

Figure 6-6

3. Pick up one blue bead and pass through the next bead from Row 2. Repeat four times. Pick up one blue bead and pass through the last bead in Row 2 and the first bead in Row 3 (**Figure 6-7**). Row 3 is now completed, six beads around.

4. Now follow the pattern in the Bead Netted Ornament design chart, adding beads as indicated for each round and passing through the beads of the previous row. Weave in the ends after the last round.

5. Carefully pass the wire through the center bead in each three-bead set on the last row. When the

wires meet, adjust the wire to make a smooth circle. Then bend the ends up (**Figure 6-8**) with the flat nosed pliers and bend one end so it has a 1/8-inch neck.

6. Grab the end with two bends with the round nosed pliers (**Figure 6-9**) and make a loop.

7. Grab the loop and the straight end with the flat nosed pliers and grab the end of the loop with the round nosed pliers; wind three times around the neck of both ends (**Figure 6-10**). Cut both ends.

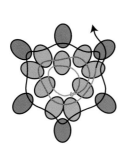

Figure 6-7

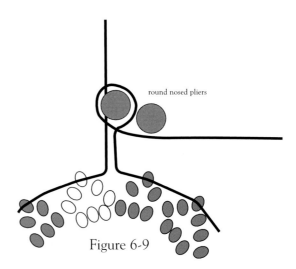

Figure 6-9

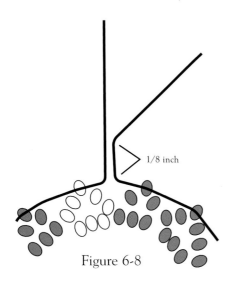

Figure 6-8

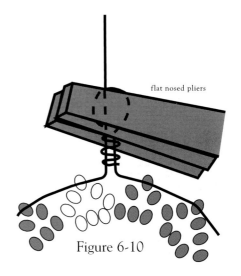

Figure 6-10

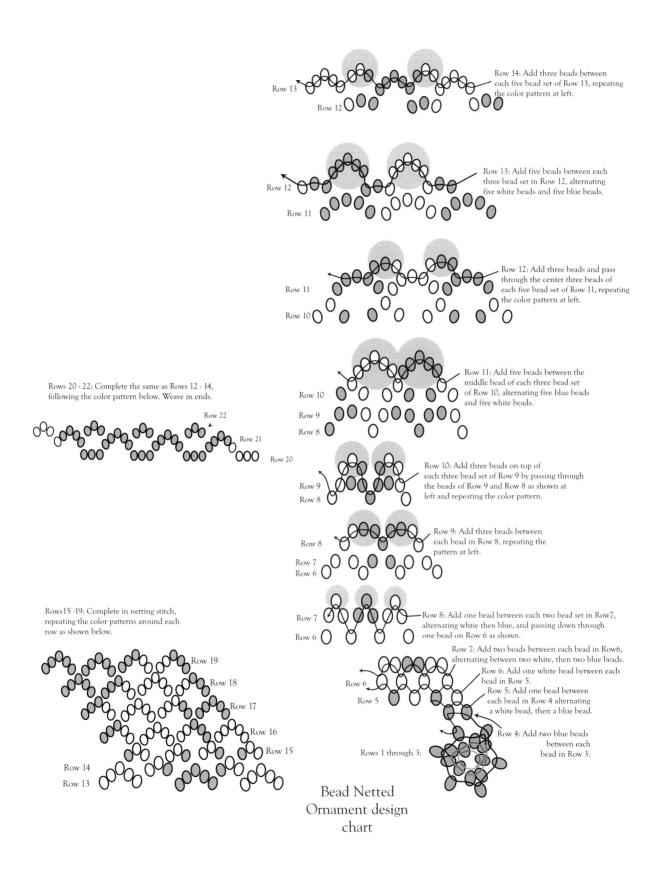

Row 13

Row 12

Row 14: Add three beads between each five bead set of Row 13, repeating the color pattern at left.

Row 12

Row 11

Row 13: Add five beads between each three bead set in Row 12, alternating five white beads and five blue beads.

Row 11

Row 10

Row 12: Add three beads and pass through the center three beads of each five bead set of Row 11, repeating the color pattern at left.

Rows 20 - 22: Complete the same as Rows 12 - 14, following the color pattern below. Weave in ends.

Row 22

Row 21

Row 20

Row 10

Row 9

Row 8

Row 11: Add five beads between the middle bead of each three bead set of Row 10, alternating five blue beads and five white beads.

Row 9

Row 8

Row 10: Add three beads on top of each three bead set of Row 9 by passing through the beads of Row 9 and Row 8 as shown at left and repeating the color pattern.

Row 8

Row 7

Row 6

Row 9: Add three beads between each bead in Row 8, repeating the pattern at left.

Rows 15 -19: Complete in netting stitch, repeating the color patterns around each row as shown below.

Row 7

Row 6

Row 8: Add one bead between each two bead set in Row7, alternating whtie then blue, and passing down through one bead on Row 6 as shown.

Row 7: Add two beads between each bead in Row6, alternating between two white, then two blue beads.

Row 6

Row 5

Row 6: Add one white bead between each bead in Row 5.

Row 5: Add one bead between each bead in Row 4 alternating a white bead, then a blue bead.

Row 19

Row 18

Row 17

Row 16

Row 15

Row 14

Row 13

Rows 1 through 3:

Row 4: Add two blue beads between each bead in Row 3.

Bead Netted
Ornament design
chart

Photo by Paul Tatingo

Circling in the Fourth Dimension, by Marlin Beads. An elegant neckpiece can be fashioned by creating a textural cord with a Zepher brand glass art bead accent. This neck chain is stitched using the quadruple helix stitch, a variation of netting in which the loops of beads are attached to the previous row by passing through the thread between the beads, instead of passing through a bead.

Using the same basic graph as the Christmas Ornament project, a variety of designs can be achieved, like this Celtic knot pattern (Odin's Glory, by Jane Davis).

Photo by Myra Nunley

Beaded Beauty, designed and beaded by Dorianne Neuhart, uses netting to encase a Cameo.

Hollyhocks amulet bag in bead netting, designed and beaded by Jane Davis.

This lacy lamp is bead netted over a fabric shade. Designed and beaded by Delinda V. Amura.

Herringbone Stitch

erringbone stitch is also known as *Ndebele* (pronounced: en dah BELL ee) stitch, named for the South African tribe that invented and uses it extensively. It is also called herringbone because of its resemblance to the chevrons of herringbone fabric.

There are two common ways to begin this stitch:

• Start with a strip of ladder stitch in larger beads than the beads for herringbone. This makes a firm, straight beginning edge to the piece as in the Pinch Purse project (on page 60).

• Start with herringbone stitch directly. This provides a beginning edge that has the same fluid drape as the rest of the bead fabric made with herringbone stitch.

The Herringbone Stitch Sample explains the direct starting method. You string cream beads for Row 1 and blue beads for Row 2. Next, you bead the third row in herringbone stitch in green beads. The beading pulls to half the width of the strung beads of Rows 1 and 2 as the blue beads move up to sit in the second row above the cream beads. You need to leave some slack in the thread as you make the first three rows so the beads can slide into the proper position. After the fourth row, it is easy to bead herringbone stitch.

Victorian Fantasy, by Jane Davis, is a gate purse in circular netting and herringbone stitch, with the floral pattern taken from the antique purse shown on the title page.

Herringbone Stitch Sample

— *You Will Need* —	
Size 11 cream seed beads, 3-1/2 grams or 1/8 oz.	size 11 seed beads
	Size B Nymo
Small amounts of light green, blue, and purple	Size 11 beading needle

Finished size: 1-1/8 inches by 2-1/8 inches

To make the herringbone sample:

1. Thread the needle with an 8-foot length of thread. Tie a stop bead 6 inches from the tail.

2. Pick up one blue bead, then pick up five repeats of two cream beads and two blue beads. Pick up two cream beads.

3. You have 23 beads for Rows 1 and 2 of the Herringbone Sample design chart. Pick up one blue bead and one green bead. Pass back through the blue bead (**Figure 7-1**).

4. Skip the two cream beads, and pass through the next blue bead. Pick up two green beads, and pass through the next blue bead (**Figure 7-2**). Push the beads on both threads so they sit in rows of the same color (**Figure 7-3**).

5. Repeat Step 4 to the end of the strand. You have finished the first three rows.

6. Pick up one green bead and one cream bead. Pass back through the green bead you just picked up and the next green bead in the row (**Figure 7-4**).

7. Pick up two cream beads and pass through the next two green beads (**Figure 7-5**).

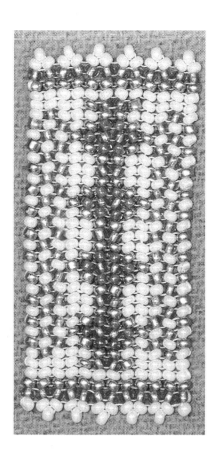

Figure 7-1

Figure 7-2

Figure 7-3

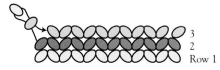

3
2
Row 1

Figure 7-4

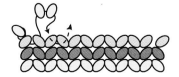

Figure 7-5

8. Continue beading as in Step 7, then turning as in Step 6, and following the color pattern in the design chart.

To add a nice finish to the ends, complete the end rows as follows:

1. On Row 1, use the tail thread and work one more row, adding one bead for each stitch instead of two.

2. On Row 33, use the working thread and work one more row, adding one bead for each stitch instead of two (**Figure 7-6**).

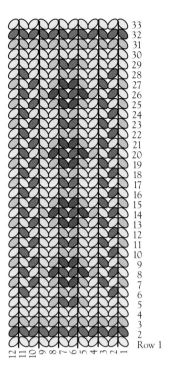

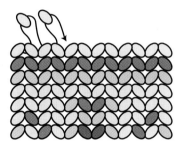

Figure 7-6

cream

green

blue

purple

Herringbone Sample

design chart

Herringbone Stitch Pinch Purse

You Will Need

Pinch purse frame, 3-1/8 inch
Size 11 seed beads, in the colors shown in the Pinch Purse design chart
42 bronze twisted bugle beads size 9 (1/8 inch long)
Brown suede: 1 piece 3-1/8 by 8 inches and 4

pieces each 1/2 by 3/4 inch
Size O brown Nymo
Size 11 beading needle
Size 12 sharps needle for sewing suede
Thimble
Knife and needle nose pliers

The soft drape of herringbone stitch makes it a good choice for purses and bags. This little pinch purse, with its curling ferns and suede lining, is as elegant as it is functional.

Finished size: 3-1/2 by 3-1/2 inches

To bead the ladder stitch and starting row:

1. Thread the beading needle with an 8-foot length of thread. Make a 42-bead ladder stitch

strip as shown on page 34, using the size 9 twisted bugle beads. Pass back through the second to last bead and make a square knot with the tail thread and working thread to hold the strip together. Pass back through the last bead.

2. Pick up bead 1 and bead 2 on Row 1 of the Pinch Purse design chart. Pass down through the second bead and up through the third bead on the ladder stitch strip (**Figure 7-7**).

3. Pick up the next two beads on Row 1 of the design chart and pass down and up through the next two ladder stitch beads.

4. Repeat Step 3 across the ladder stitch strip, following the color pattern of the design chart. One side of the first row of the purse is complete.

5. Pass through the loop between the second and third size 9 beads (**Figure 7-8**). Pass back through the last size 9 bead (**Figure 7-9**).

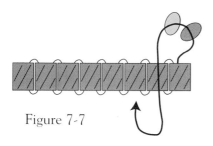

Figure 7-7

Figure 7-8

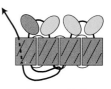

Figure 7-9

6. Repeat Steps 2 and 3 across the ladder stitch strip along the other side. Repeat Step 5.

You have finished Row 1 of the design chart once for the front and once the back of the purse. You are now ready to begin beading in the round in herringbone stitch.

To bead the herringbone stitch purse:
1. Pass up through the first bead (**Figure 7-10**). Pick up bead 1 and bead 2 in Row 2 of the design chart and pass through bead 2 and bead 3 of Row 1 (**Figure 7-11**).

2. Continue in herringbone stitch to the end of one side of the purse, then repeat the pattern on the other side. When you get to the beginning of the row, step up by finishing the last stitch and then passing through the first bead in the current row (**Figure 7-12**).

3. Continue beading, following the design chart color pattern. For the last row, add just one bead for each stitch, instead of two. This makes a nice edging. Weave in the ends.

To assemble the purse:
1. Using the knife edge, bend back the metal flap that holds the pin in the hinge on one side of the purse frame and remove the pin so the purse frame opens flat for easier assembly.
2. Cut a rectangle from each of the corners of the 8-inch long piece of suede (**Figure 7-13**).

3. Fold one short side of the 8-inch piece of suede over 3/4 inch and stitch in place (**Figure 7-14**). Repeat for the other side. Stitch 1/8 inch side seams. Slip this lining onto the purse frame, reinsert the hinge, and fold down the metal flap with the pliers.

4. Stitch the four small strips of suede to the inside and outside of the beading to pad the beading, along the sides of the purse where the hinge will be.

5. Slip the beading onto the suede lining and blind stitch to the top of the suede lining.

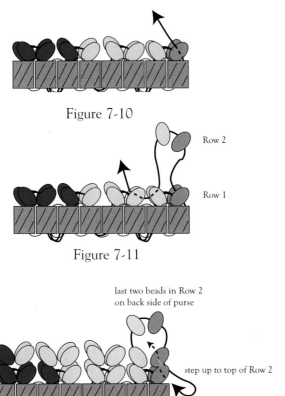

Figure 7-10

Row 2

Row 1

Figure 7-11

last two beads in Row 2
on back side of purse

step up to top of Row 2

Figure 7-12

Cut notch
1 1/2 inches long
by 1/8 inch wide
at each corner
of suede

Figure 7-13

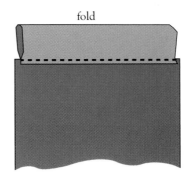

fold

Figure 7-14

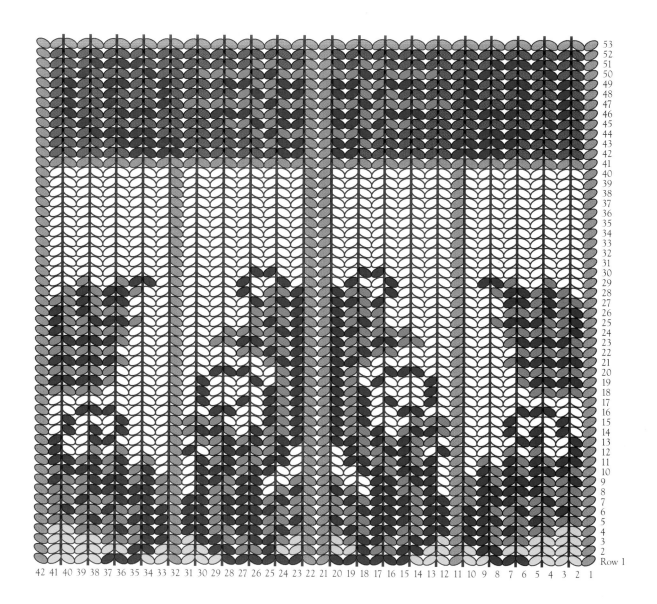

53
52
51
50
49
48
47
46
45
44
43
42
41
40
39
38
37
36
35
34
33
32
31
30
29
28
27
26
25
24
23
22
21
20
19
18
17
16
15
14
13
12
11
10
9
8
7
6
5
4
3
2
Row 1

42 41 40 39 38 37 36 35 34 33 32 31 30 29 28 27 26 25 24 23 22 21 20 19 18 17 16 15 14 13 12 11 10 9 8 7 6 5 4 3 2 1

Dull white, 20 grams or 3/4 oz.

Lime green, 10 grams or 3/8 oz.

Hunter green, 10 grams or 3/8 oz.

Mustard, 1 gram

Bronze, 10 grams or 3/8 oz.

Matte brown, 5 grams or 3/16 oz.

Pinch Purse
design chart

Chapter 8

Right-angle Weave

Right-angle weave is an old beading technique commonly done around the world with two needles. The single-needle version popularized in the United States by bead artist David Chatt uses a figure-eight thread path to hold beads together in a square grid. The single-needle version is explained in this book.

The name right-angle weave describes the stitch: beads are placed at right angles to each other. Because the needle is first going clockwise to put on a set of beads, then counterclockwise to put on the next set of beads, this is a difficult stitch to work correctly at first. But, once you get the rhythm of the turns, it becomes a fun stitch to bead.

You start with a square of four beads. Make the first row by adding three beads to the end of the four-bead square, then passing through the beads to come out of the center bead of the three beads. Then, you add another three-bead set and continue connecting squares in a row. You work the following rows by attaching to the first row to make a grid of interconnected four-bead squares.

Because the thread goes through the beads several times, it is important to use a thinner thread and beads with large, regular holes.

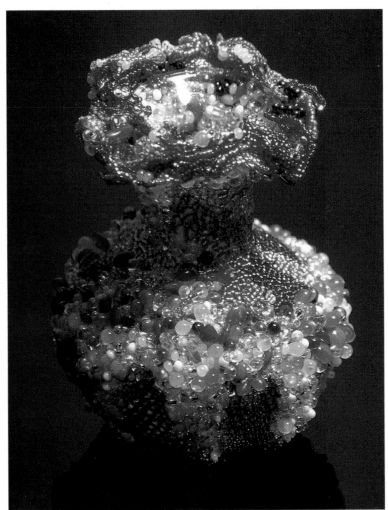

Right-angle weave and a variety of bead types add texture to this piece, by Susan Hilyar.

This intricate design, by Marlin Beads, combines several stitches, including right-angle weave, to make a fun, complex piece.

Right-angle Weave Sample

You Will Need

Size 11 cream seed beads, 3-1/2 grams or 1/8 oz.

Small amounts of green, pink, purple, and blue size 11 seed beads

Size B Nymo

Size 11 beading needle

Finished size: 1-1/8 inches by 2-1/8 inches

1. Thread the needle with an 8-foot length of thread. Pick up four cream beads and tie the tail and working thread into a square knot 6 inches from the tail. Pass through one bead. These are the first four beads of Row 1 on the Right-angle Weave Sample design chart.

2. Pick up three cream beads and pass through the bead the thread is coming out of and through two beads of the three-bead set (**Figure 8-1**).

3. Pick up three cream beads and pass through the bead the thread is coming out of and through two beads of the three-bead set (**Figure 8-2**).

4. Repeat Steps 2 and 3 three more times. You have nine interconnected squares making up the first row on the design chart.

lighter beads show current stitch

Figure 8-1

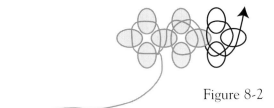

Figure 8-2

5. Pass through the next bead, pick up three cream beads, and pass through the bead the thread is coming out of and through the first of the three beads just strung (**Figure 8-3**).

6. At the beginning of each row, you put on three beads at a time to make the turns. You put on two beads at a time for the rest of the row.

7. Pick up two cream beads and pass through the beads as shown (**Figure 8-4**).

8. Pick up two cream beads and pass through the beads as shown (**Figure 8-5**).

9. Repeat Steps 6 and 7 across the row. Turn as in Step 5. Two rows are completed.

10. Continue in right-angle weave, adding beads and following the color sequence from the design chart. Weave in the ends.

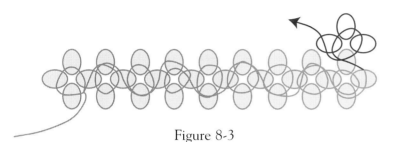

Figure 8-3

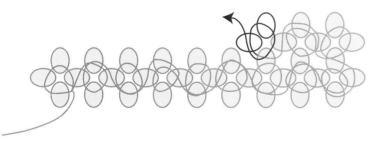

Figure 8-4

Figure 8-5

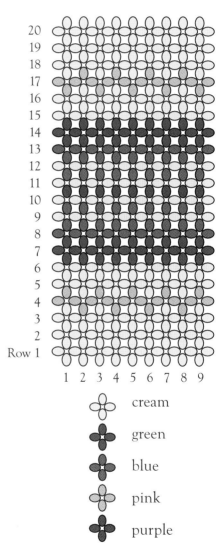

Right-angle Weave Sample design chart

Right-angle Weave   67

Right-angle Weave Band on a Wicker Basket

You Will Need

11-1/2-inch diameter wicker basket with at least a 3-inch section of straight sides
Size 6 seed beads, 16 oz. of cream and 8 oz. of green
Size 8 DMC brown pearl cotton to match the basket color
Size 10 beading needle
Beeswax
Rubber band large enough to go around the basket or 2 feet of elastic

Large beads and a meandering vine design complement the rough woven texture of this basket. To prevent the pearl cotton from fraying as it slides through the beads, wax it well. The thick pearl cotton fills the holes of the large beads, keeping the correct tension in this loose stitch.

Finished size: 3-inch wide band around an 11-1/2-inch diameter basket

1. Cut a 9-foot length of pearl cotton, apply beeswax, and thread the needle.

2. Following the Beaded Band design chart, bead the pattern twice in flat right-angle weave, following the instructions from the Right-angle Weave Sample (on page 66).

3. Join the first and last rows together by adding one bead at a time, maintaining the color pattern and passing through beads from each end (**Figure 8-6**). Weave in the ends.

4. Slip the beadwork on the basket and hold in place with a large rubber band or a piece of elastic thread to tie the beadwork to the basket.

5. Sew the beadwork to the basket along the top edge first, passing through an edge bead and then through the weave of the basket.

6. Remove the elastic or rubber band and stitch the bottom edge of the beadwork to the basket the same as for the top.

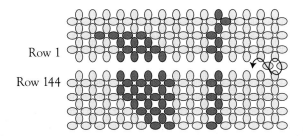

Row 1

Row 144

Figure 8-6

Beaded Band
design chart

cream

green

Chapter 9
Knitting

Techniques for Prestrung Beads

To work beads into a crocheted, knitted, or tatted project, you must string the beads on the thread first. This means that you have no loose beads to worry about and can take projects that use prestrung beads on trips with ease. Because it is important to string all of the beads in the correct color order, the preparation for starting these project takes extra time and careful attention.

Note: For the techniques in Chapters 9 through 11, you will require a previous knowledge of knitting, crochet, and tatting.

Basic Techniques for Stringing Beads

To Slide Prestrung Beads on Project Thread or Yarn
This technique is used when you have purchased beads in hanks and all of the beads in the project are the same.

1. Pull one strand of beads from the hank and tie a knot around the bead at one end of the strand to prevent the beads from falling off.
2. Tie an overhand knot at the other end of the strand around the project thread or yarn so that the project thread or yarn folds in half inside the knot.
3. Carefully slide about 1 inch of beads at a time from one thread to the other. This takes some practice. The thread used for bead hanks is easily broken if you pull hard; the knot may get loose and your project thread can slip out. Beads that are misshapen or with holes that are too small to slide over the knot have to be discarded. When any of these problems occur, if there are still plenty of beads on the strand, retie the strand to the project thread and continue sliding the beads.

To String Beads Following a Design
If the beads are not in hanks, or they need to be strung in a color order according to a design, use a needle small enough to fit through the bead holes. If the project thread is too thick to fit the bead needle, tie a 10-inch piece of beading thread to the project thread and thread the needle with the beading

Correcting Errors

Beads in the Wrong Place
If a bead is knit into, or between, the wrong stitches, it must be removed or reworked. If all of the beads are one color, you can break the bead, if it is an extra bead; otherwise, you must rip back to that section and knit or crochet it again. For tatting, it's best just to cut it out and redo the section. Make sure to take your time and carefully check each row or section before beginning the next.

Beads in the Wrong Color Sequence
Because the beads in a color pattern are all strung in a specific order, it's very important to work each row correctly, because any error will throw off the pattern for the rest of the work. Always check the pattern after knitting or crocheting each row to make sure you have completed the row correctly. Knitting or crocheting a pattern using paper row markers helps you find errors quickly. If you get to the end of a row and have beads left over, or you get to the marker and haven't finished the row, you know you have made a mistake. (For example, you may have strung the wrong number of beads for that row, or stitched too many or too few into the row.) Correct the error before continuing, then tear off the row marker and begin the next row.

thread, or use a wire needle with a collapsing eye (**Figure 9-1**).

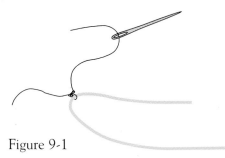

Figure 9-1

String the beads according to the design chart. When stringing beads following a design chart, separate each row with a small piece of paper. This helps you in double-checking for errors. I use 3/8-inch squares of paper I have already pierced with a large needle so that they fit easily over the needle and thread or yarn.

To Clear the Working Thread

About every four rows, you will use up the yarn or thread and need to slide the beads away from the project to clear some more thread to continue. Keep the thread ball in a basket and slide about 4 to 6 inches of beads along the yarn or thread at a time, until there are about 4 feet of yarn or thread without beads near your project. If you have beads for a row in progress, leave those up near the work.

To Keep Track of Beads Per Row

In patterns where the bead count changes from row to row, the number in parentheses following the row number tells you how many beads are needed for the row. Slide that number of beads up near your project before beginning each row. The paper row marker makes this easy to find.

To Attach New Thread or Yarn

When you run out of beads or thread, or need to correct a stringing error, you will need to attach a new thread.
• In knitting, change at the end of a row.
• In tatting, change threads after a ring.
• In crochet, anywhere is okay.
• Cut the working thread to about 6 inches.
• For knitting and tatting, tie the tail and new thread into a knot as close to the work as possible.
• For crochet, pull a loop of the new thread through

the loop on the hook and pull the old thread as tight as possible.
• Continue working as before using the new thread.
• When the piece is finished, bury the ends into the back of the work for about 1-1/2 inches and cut the excess yarn or thread.

Knitting

There are two types of knitting with beads, both of which you will use in this book.

Beaded Knitting

For this type, one or more beads are slid between stitches on the thread or yarn. The bead lies on the front or back of the knitting based on the stitches beside it. A bead bordered by knit stitches lies on the back of the fabric, while purl stitches on either side of the bead cause it to stay on the front of the fabric. The beads lie horizontally in the fabric, or hang in a swag or loop if many beads are slid between stitches.

Bead Knitting

Here, a bead is pushed into a stitch as it is made. This technique is more difficult than beaded knitting, because there must be tension on the thread and the bead must be positioned properly so it can be pushed into the stitch. It was traditionally accomplished in twisted stockinette stitch and more recently in plaited stockinette stitch. These tight stitches are needed so that the knitting locks the beads on the right side of the fabric.

Twisted stockinette stitch: All of the stitches are made by knitting into the back of the stitch. This technique causes all of the beads to slant in the same direction and the fabric to have a strong bias slant.

Plaited stockinette stitch: The knit stitches are made by knitting into the back of the stitch and wrapping the thread or yarn clockwise around the needle. The purl stitches are made by purling into the front of the stitch and wrapping the thread or yarn counterclockwise around the needle (standard purl stitch). The beads alternately slant to the right in one row, and then to the left in the next, and the finished fabric has no bias slant. Plaited bead knitting was developed in the 1980s by Alice Korach, the founder of *Bead & Button Magazine*. It is the technique used for projects in this book.

Bead-knitted scarf, designed and knitted by Jane Davis for Linda Niemeyer and Blue Sky Alpacas, using size 6 pearl beads, size 5 knitting needles, and sport-weight Blue Sky Alpacas alpaca yarn. Pattern available from Blue Sky Alpacas (see Supply Sources).

Beaded Knitting Sample

You Will Need
---

300 size 11 cream seed beads
Size 12 cream pearl cotton

Size 000 or 0000 knitting needles
Size 11 beading needle

Finished size: 1 inch by 1-3/4 inches at the widest point

Note: You may wish to practice first with size 6 beads using a sport-weight yarn and size 5 knitting needles. It takes time to get used to the small needles.

String the beads onto the pearl cotton.
Cast on 12 stitches.
Rows 1-3: Knit.
Row 4: Knit two stitches, slide one bead next to the second stitch, knit two more stitches, and slide one bead next to the second stitch. Repeat the pattern to the end of the row, knitting the last two stitches.
Rows 5-7: Knit the same as Row 4.
Rows 8-11: Knit the same as Row 4 except slide two beads between the stitches instead of one.
Rows 12-22: Knit the same as the previous rows, increasing the number of beads between stitches by one every four rows.

To cast off on row 23, slide five beads up to the needle. Cut the thread 12 inches from the beads and thread the beading needle. Pass through the first two stitches and slide them off of the knitting needle. Pick up five beads, slide them next to the knitting, and pass the beading needle through the next two stitches, sliding them off of the knitting needle. Repeat to the end. Weave in the tail thread.

You Will Need

Size 11 seed beads, in the colors shown in
the Bead Knitting Sample design chart
Size 8 cream pearl cotton or size 20 cream

Cebelia
Size 000 or 0000 knitting needles
Size 11 or medium wire beading needle

Finished size: 1-1/8 inches by 2-1/8 inches

Note: You may wish to practice first with size 6
beads using a sport-weight yarn and size 5 knitting
needles. It takes time to get used to the small needles.

Beginning at the top row, string the beads onto
the thread from right to left or left to right (the
design is symmetrical), following the Bead
Knitting Sample design chart.
Cast on 24 stitches.
Row 1: Knit into the back of each stitch, wrapping
the thread or yarn around the needle clockwise.
Row 2: Purl two stitches, then purl the next
stitch, sliding a bead into the stitch as it is made.

To put a bead in a purl stitch:

1. Keeping the tension tight on the thread, insert
the right needle into the front of the stitch on the
left needle as to purl.

2. Slide one bead about 3/8 inch (about 1/2 inch
for size 8 or size 6 beads) from the stitch. Wrap
the thread or yarn around the right needle counterclockwise.

3. Pull the right needle toward you and the left
needle away from you to create a gap between the
stitch, and slide the bead through the gap to the
right side of the knitting (facing away from you).

4. Finish the stitch.

Bead purl the next 21 stitches. Purl the last two
stitches.

Row 3: Knit two stitches. Knit the next stitch,
sliding a bead into the stitch as it is made.

To put a bead in a knit stitch:

1. Keeping the tension tight on the thread, insert
the right needle into the back of the stitch on the
left needle as to knit.

2. Slide one bead about 3/8 inch (about 1/2 inch
for size 8 or size 6 beads) from the stitch. Wrap
the yarn around the right needle clockwise.

3. Pull the right needle toward you and the left
needle away from you to create a gap between the
stitch, and slide the bead through the gap to the
right side of the knitting (facing you).

4. Finish the stitch.

Bead knit the next 21 stitches. Knit the last two
stitches.

Rows 4-9: Repeat Rows 2 and 3 above.
Row 10: Purl. Cast off.

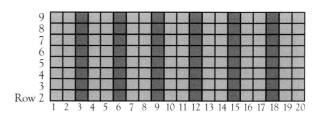

Bead Knitting Sample
design chart

☐ light blue

■ blue

Beaded Knitting Pillow

You Will Need

2 skeins of Crème Brulee by Knit One
   Crochet Two (each approx. 50 grams, or
   131 yards or 120 meters), 100% wool, color
   #294
40 grams or 1-1/2 oz. size 6 pearl-toned beads
Size 5 circular knitting needle, 24 inches or
   60cm long

Size F and I crochet hooks
Size 10 beading needle and 10 inches of beading thread to string beads on yarn
21 inches by 16-1/2 inches cotton fabric to
   blend with the yarn color
Stuffing

Making a pillow is a great way to try a new technique; it is small enough to complete easily, yet large enough to get comfortable with the technique.

Here is a quick project to get you accustomed to knitting with beads. I was inspired by the small repeating patterns of Fair Isle knits from the Shetland Islands and the rich cable textures of Aran sweaters of the Aran Isles.

Only the front of the pillow is knitted, then you sew it to a fabric pillow casing and stuff. You will be knitting flat, alternately using one skein strung with beads and one skein without beads. This minimizes wear on the yarn from sliding the beads. Circular needles are used so you can pick up the type of yarn you need at the beginning of either end of the row.

Finished size: 10 inches by 15-1/2 inches

String all of the beads onto one skein of yarn. Using the non-beaded skein, cast on 80 sts. The numbers in parenthesis at the beginning of the row are the total number of beads you will knit in that row.

Row 1: (0) (K1, P1) repeat across
Row 2: (0) (P1, K1) repeat across
Rows 3-8: alternate Row 1 and Row 2
Row 9: (0) (K1, P1) x 3, K68, (K1, P1) x 3
Row 10: (0) (P1, K1) x 3, P68, (P1, K1) x 3
Row 11: (0) (K1, P1) x 3, K68, (K1, P1) x 3
Row 12: (0) (P1, K1) x 3, K68, (P1, K1) x 3
Row 13: (0) (K1, P1) x 3, K68, (K1, P1) x 3
Attach and begin using beaded yarn.
Row 14: (17) (P1, K1) x 3, K2, B, (K4, B) x 16, K2, (P1, K1) x 3
Row 15: (51) (K1, P1) x 3, (P1, B, P1, B, P1, B, P1) x 17, (K1, P1) x 3
Row 16: (17) (P1, K1) x 3, K2, B, (K4, B) x 16, K2, (P1, K1) x 3
Begin at the opposite end of needle, using non-beaded yarn.
Row 17: (0) (K1, P1) x 3, P68, (K1, P1) x 3
Row 18: (0) (P1, K1) x 3, P68, (P1, K1) x 3
Row 19: (0) (K1, P1) x 3, P68, (K1, P1) x 3
Change to beaded yarn.
Row 20: (33) (P1, K1) x 3, (P2, B) x 33, P2, (P1, K1) x 3
Begin at the opposite end of the needle, using non-beaded yarn.
Row 21: (0) (K1, P1) x 3, K68, (K1, P1) x 3
Row 22: (0) (P1, K1) x 3, K68, (P1, K1) x 3
Row 23: (0) (K1, P1) x 3, K68, (K1, P1) x 3
Change to beaded yarn.
Row 24: (17) (P1, K1) x 3, (P2, K1, B, K1) x 17, (P1, K1) x 3
Row 25: (17) (K1, P1) x 3, K1, P1, B, P1, (K2, P1, B, P1) x 16, K1, (K1, P1) x 3
Row 26: (17) (P1, K1) x 3, (K1, B, K1, P2) x 17, (P1, K1) x 3
Begin at the opposite end of the needle, using non-beaded yarn.
Row 27: (0) (K1, P1) x 3, P68, (K1, P1) x 3
Row 28: (0) (P1, K1) x 3, P68, (P1, K1) x 3
Row 29: (0) (K1, P1) x 3, P68, (K1, P1) x 3
Row 30: (0) (P1, K1) x 3, K68, (P1, K1) x 3
Row 31: (0) (K1, P1) x 3, P68, (K1, P1) x 3
Row 32: (0) (P1, K1) x 3, P68, (P1, K1) x 3

Row 33: (0) (K1, P1) x 3, P68, (K1, P1) x 3
Change to beaded yarn.
Row 34: (14) (P1, K1) x 3, (P1, B, P1, K3) x 13, P1, B, P1, K1, (P1, K1) x 3
Row 35: (14) (K1, P1) x 3, P1, (K1, B, K1, P3) x 13, K1, B, K1, (K1, P1) x 3
Row 36: (14) (P1, K1) x 3, (P1, B, P1, K3) x 13, P1, B, P1, K1, (P1, K1) x 3
Row 37: (27) (K1, P1) x 3, (K1, B, K2, B, K1, P1) x 13, K1, B, K2, (K1, P1) x 3
Row 38: (67) (P1, K1) x 3, (P1, B) x 67, P1, (P1, K1) x 3
Row 39: (40) (K1, P1) x 3, P1, K1, (B, K2, B, K1, B, K2) x 13, B, K1, (K1, P1) x 3
Row 40: (27) (P1, K1) x 3, P2, B, P1, (K1, P1, B, P2, B, P1) x 13, (P1, K1) x 3
Row 41: (14) (K1, P1) x 3, P1, (K1, B, K1, P3) x 13, K1, B, K1, (K1, P1) x 3
Change to non-beaded yarn.
Row 42: (0) (P1, K1) x 3, K68, (P1, K1) x 3
Row 43: (0) (K1, P1) x 3, K68, (K1, P1) x 3
Row 44: (0) (P1, K1) x 3, K68, (P1, K1) x 3
Row 45: (0) (K1, P1) x 3, P68, (K1, P1) x 3
Row 46: (0) (P1, K1) x 3, K68, (P1, K1) x 3
Row 47: (0) (K1, P1) x 3, K68, (K1, P1) x 3
Row 48: (0) (P1, K1) x 3, K68, (P1, K1) x 3
Begin at the opposite end of the needle, using beaded yarn.
Row 49: (14) (K1, P1) x 3, (P1, B, P1, K3) x 13, P1, B, P1, (K1, P1) x 3
Row 50: (27) (P1, K1) x 3, (K1, B, K2, B, K1, P1) x 13, K1, B, K2, (P1, K1) x 3
Begin at the opposite end of the needle, using non-beaded yarn.
Row 51: (0) (K1, P1) x 3, P68, (K1, P1) x 3
Row 52: (0) (P1, K1) x 3, P68, (P1, K1) x 3
Row 53: (0) (K1, P1) x 3, P68, (K1, P1) x 3
Change to beaded yarn.
Row 54: (13) (P1, K1) x 3, P1, (B, P1, K7, P1, B, P1) x 6, B, P1, K6, (P1, K1) x 3
Row 55: (13) (K1, P1) x 3, (P5, K1, B, K2, B, K1) x 6, P5, K1, B, K1, P1, (K1, P1) x 3
Row 56: (13) (P1, K1) x 3, K2, (P1, B, P1, K3) x 13, P1, (P1, K1) x 3
Row 57: (14) (K1, P1) x 3, K1, B, K1, P1, K1, B, K1, P5) x 6, K1, B, K1, P1, K1, B, K1, P3, (K1, P1) x 3
Row 58: (14) (P1, K1) x 3, K4, (P1, B, P1, B, P1, K7) x 6, P1, B, P1, B, P1, K1, (P1, K1) x 3

Begin at the opposite end of the needle, using non-beaded yarn.

Row 59: (0) (K1, P1) x 3, K68, (K1, P1) x 3
Row 60: (0) (P1, K1) x 3, K68, (P1, K1) x 3
Row 61: (0) (K1, P1) x 3, K68, (K1, P1) x 3
Change to beaded yarn.
Row 62: (13) (P1, K1) x 3, (P3, K1, B, K1) x 13, P3, (P1, K1) x 3
Row 63: (39) (K1, P1) x 3, K2, (P1, B, P1, B, P1, B, P1, K1) x 13, K2, (K1, P1) x 3
Row 64: (39) (P1, K1) x 3, P2, (K1, B, K1, B, K1, B, K1, P1) x 13, P2, (P1, K1) x 3
Row 65: (13) (K1, P1) x 3, (K3, P1, B, P1) x 13, K3, (K1, P1) x 3
Change to non-beaded yarn.
Row 66: (0) (P1, K1) x 3, P68, (P1, K1) x 3
Row 67: (0) (K1, P1) x 3, P68, (K1, P1) x 3
Row 68: (0) (P1, K1) x 3, P68, (P1, K1) x 3
Row 69: (0) (K1, P1) x 3, K68, (K1, P1) x 3
Row 70: (0) (P1, K1) x 3, P68, (P1, K1) x 3
Row 71: (0) (K1, P1) x 3, P68, (K1, P1) x 3
Row 72: (0) (P1, K1) x 3, P68, (P1, K1) x 3
Begin at the opposite end of the needle, using beaded yarn.
Row 73: (17) (K1, P1) x 3, K2, B, (K4, B) x 16, K2, (K1, P1) x 3
Change to non-beaded yarn.
Row 74: (0) (P1, K1) x 3, K68, (P1, K1) x 3
Row 75: (0) (K1, P1) x 3, K68, (K1, P1) x 3
Row 76: (0) (P1, K1) x 3, K68, (P1, K1) x 3
Row 77: (0) (K1, P1) x 3, P68, (K1, P1) x 3
Row 78: (0) (P1, K1) x 3, K68, (P1, K1) x 3
Rows 79-86: (0) Same as Rows 1-8

Bind off loosely.
Block to 10 inches x 15-1/2 inches. Weave in the tails and working yarn.

To make a crocheted edging for pillow:

1. Using one strand of yarn and the size F crochet hook, single crochet loosely around the edges of the knitting, making three single crochet in the corners.

2. Using two strands of yarn and the size I crochet hook, single crochet, loosely, backwards into every other single crochet stitch. At each corner, single crochet in the two stitches before and after the corner stitch.

To make the pillow casing:

1. Fold the fabric, right sides together, to 10-1/2 inches x 16-1/2 inches.

2. Stitch the edges using a 1/2-inch seam allowance, leaving a 4-inch gap on the 16-1/2-inch edge for filling with stuffing. Clip corners, turn right side out, and press.

3. Stitch the knitting to one side of the pillow so that the crochet edging extends beyond the pillow edge.

4. Stuff the pillow and whip stitch the opening closed.

Blue Thistle Beaded Purse

You Will Need

3-inch clasp as pictured, inside dimensions, closed: 2-1/4 inches x 1-1/8 inches

60 yards of YLI silk cord 1000 denier, Corn Flower Blue

2 hanks of blue pearlized size 11 seed beads

Size 11 white pearl-toned seed beads, 4 grams or 1/8 oz.

Size 000 or 0000 double pointed knitting needles

Size 10 or 11 beading needle

This little purse uses the knitting techniques of the antique beaded purses made at the turn of the nineteenth century. The thistle pattern idea at the top is a new touch I added to update this style.

Finished size: 5 inches x 4 inches at the widest point

Slide seven strands of the blue beads onto the silk cord. Thread the needle and string the thistle pattern on the Blue Thistle Beaded Purse design chart, from Row 12 to Row 1, right to left or left to right (the design is symmetrical), separating each row with a small piece of paper.

Cast on 32 stitches.
Row 1: Knit
Row 2: Knit
Row 3: K4, (B1, K1) x 25, K3
Row 4: Knit
Row 5: K3, (B1, K1) x 27, K2
Rows 6-26: alternate Rows 4 and 5
The thistle pattern is completed. Only blue beads remain on the silk cord.
Rows 27 and 28: K2, (B1, K2) x 15
Rows 29 and 30: K2, (B1, K2, B2, K2) x 7, B2, K2
Rows 31 and 32: K2, (B1, K2, B3, K2) x 7, B1, K2
Rows 33 and 34: K2, (B1, K2, B4, K2, B1, K2, B2, K2) x 3, B1, K2, B4, K2, B1, K2

Rows 35 and 36: K2, (B1, K2, B5, K2, B1, K2, B1, K2) x 3, B1, K2, B5, K2, B1, K2
Rows 37 and 38: K2, (B1, K2, B6, K2, B1, K2, B1, K2) x 3, B1, K2, B6, K2, B1, K2
Rows 39 and 40: K2, (B1, K2, B6, K2, B1, K2, B2, K2) x 3, B1, K2, B6, K2, B1, K2
Rows 41 and 42: K2, (B1, K2, B5, K2, B1, K2, B3, K2) x 3, B1, K2, B5, K2, B1, K2
Rows 43 and 44: K2, (B1, K2, B4, K2) x 7, B1, K2
Rows 45 and 46: K2, (B1, K2, B3, K2, B1, K2, B5, K2) x 3, B1, K2, B3, K2, B1, K2
Rows 47 and 48: K2, (B1, K2, B2, K2, B1, K2, B6,

K2) x 3, B1, K2, B2, K2, B1, K2

Rows 49 and 50: K2, (B1, K2, B1, K2, B1, K2, B7, K2) x 3, B1, K2, B1, K2, B1, K2

Rows 51 and 52: K2, (B1, K2, B2, K2, B1, K2, B7, K2) x 3, B1, K2, B2, K2, B1, K2

Rows 53 and 54: K2, (B1, K2, B3, K2, B1, K2, B6, K2) x 3, B1, K2, B3, K2, B1, K2

Rows 55 and 56: K2, (B1, K2, B4, K2, B1, K2, B5, K2) x 3, B1, K2, B4, K2, B1, K2

Rows 57 and 58: K2, (B1, K2, B5, K2, B1, K2, B4, K2) x 3, B1, K2, B5, K2, B1, K2

Rows 59 and 60: K2, (B1, K2, B6, K2, B1, K2, B3, K2) x 3, B1, K2, B6, K2, B1, K2

Rows 61 and 62: K2, (B1, K2, B7, K2, B1, K2, B2, K2) x 3, B1, K2, B7, K2, B1, K2

Rows 63 and 64: K2, (B1, K2, B8, K2, B1, K2, B1, K2) x 3, B1, K2, B8, K2, B1, K2

Rows 65 and 66: K2, (B1, K2, B8, K2, B1, K2, B1, K2) x 3, B1, K2, B8, K2, B1, K2

Rows 67 and 68: K2, (B1, K2, B7, K2, B1, K2, B2, K2) x 3, B1, K2, B7, K2, B1, K2

Rows 69 and 70: K2, (B1, K2, B6, K2, B1, K2, B3, K2) x 3, B1, K2, B6, K2, B1, K2

Rows 71 and 72: K2, (B1, K2, B5, K2, B1, K2, B4, K2) x 3, B1, K2, B5, K2, B1, K2

Rows 73 and 74: K2, (B1, K2, B4, K2, B1, K2, B5, K2) x 3, B1, K2, B4, K2, B1, K2

Rows 75 and 76: K2, (B1, K2, B3, K2, B1, K2, B6, K2) x 3, B1, K2, B3, K2, B1, K2

Rows 77 and 78: K2, (B1, K2, B2, K2, B1, K2, B7, K2) x 3, B1, K2, B2, K2, B1, K2

Rows 79 and 80: K2, (B1, K2, B1, K2, B1, K2, B8, K2) x 3, B1, K2, B1, K2, B1, K2

Rows 81 and 82: K2, (B1, K2, B1, K2, B1, K2, B8, K2) x 3, B1, K2, B1, K2, B1, K2

Rows 83 and 84: K2, (B1, K2, B2, K2, B1, K2, B7, K2) x 3, B1, K2, B2, K2, B1, K2

Rows 85 and 86: K2, (B1, K2, B3, K2, B1, K2, B6, K2) x 3, B1, K2, B3, K2, B1, K2

Rows 87 and 88: K2, (B1, K2, B4, K2, B1, K2, B5, K2) x 3, B1, K2, B4, K2, B1, K2

Rows 89 and 90: K2, (B1, K2, B5, K2, B1, K2, B4, K2) x 3, B1, K2, B5, K2, B1, K2

Rows 91 and 92: K2, (B1, K2, B6, K2, B1, K2, B3, K2) x 3, B1, K2, B6, K2, B1, K2

Rows 93 and 94: K2, (B1, K2, B7, K2, B1, K2, B2, K2) x 3, B1, K2, B7, K2, B1, K2

Rows 95 and 96: K2, (B1, K2, B8, K2, B1, K2, B1, K2) x 3, B1, K2, B8, K2, B1, K2

Rows 97 and 98: K2, (B1, K2, B9, K2, B1, K2, B1, K2) x 3, B1, K2, B9, K2, B1, K2

Rows 99 and 100: K2, (B1, K2, B10, K2, B1, K2, B1, K2) x 3, B1, K2, B10, K2, B1, K2

Rows 101 and 102: K2, (B1, K2, B10, K2, B1, K2, B1, K2) x 3, B1, K2, B10, K2, B1, K2

Rows 103 and 104: K2, (B1, K2, B10, K2, B1, K2, B1, K2) x 3, B1, K2, B10, K2, B1, K2

This is one half of the bag. To make the other half, continue knitting, following the directions in reverse order from Row 98 to Row 27. Cut the silk cord 6 inches from the knitting. Thread the needle onto a new silk cord and string the thistle pattern on the design chart, from Row 12 to Row 1, right to left or left to right. Attach to the knitting and knit one row, then knit following the instructions for Row 26 to Row 1 in reverse order. Bind off. Weave in the ends.

Finishing:
Carefully stitch each end of the bag to the sew holes in the clasp, pulling tight to hide the holes. Stitch the sides together, beginning 3/8 inch below the sew holes for the clasp hinge to open and close.

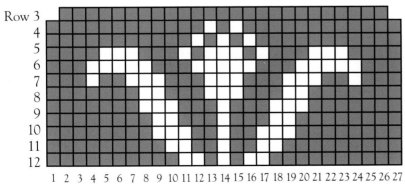

Blue Thistle Beaded Purse

design chart

☐ white

▨ blue

Daisy Scissors Case

You Will Need

1 ball #8 DMC pearl cotton in a color to match the background beads
Size 000 or 0000 knitting needles
Size 11 seed beads, in the colors shown in the Daisy Scissors Case design chart
1 large oval bead for the closure
Scraps of suede to fit the lining patterns in

Figure 9-2
Leather needle
Beading needle
Thimble (for pushing the needles through the leather)
Size 0 beading thread

This scissors case is easier to make than it looks. Once you string the beads accurately onto the pearl cotton, you can enjoy the project. If you haven't worked with such small needles before, knit a small practice swatch, with or without beads. If you like to knit, you will enjoy this once you get the hang of the beads and needles.

Knitting the back:

Following the pattern in the Daisy Scissors Case design chart, string the size 11 seed beads beginning at Row 90, and working down to Row 4, from either left to right or right to left (the design is symmetrical) onto the pearl cotton. The design chart only shows the bead pattern of the scissors case. The first three rows of knitting do not have beads and are not shown on the design chart, nor are two stitches on the sides of the chart.

Cast on 8 sts
Row 1: knit
Row 2: purl
Row 3: knit
Row 4: P2, PB4, P2
Row 5: K2, KB5, inc 1. 9 sts total
Row 6: P2, PB6, inc 1. 10 sts total
Row 7: K2, KB7, inc 1. 11 sts total
Row 8: P2, PB8, inc 1. 12 sts total

Row 9: K2, KB9, inc 1. 13 sts total
Row 10: P2, PB10, inc 1. 14 sts total
Row 11: K3, KB9, K2
Row 12: P2, PB10, P2
Row 13: K2, KB11, inc 1. 15 sts total
Row 14: P2, PB12, inc 1. 16 sts total
Row 15: K2, KB13, inc 1. 17 sts total

Row 16: P2, PB14, inc 1. 18 sts total
Row 17: K3, KB13, K2
Row 18: P2, PB14, P2
Row 19: K2, KB15, inc 1. 19 sts total
Row 20: P2, PB16, inc 1. 20 sts total
Row 21: K3, KB15, K2
Row 22: P2, PB16, P2
Row 23: K2, KB17, inc 1. 21 sts total
Row 24: P3, PB16, P2
Row 25: K2, KB17, K2
Row 26: P2, PB18, inc 1. 22 sts total
Row 27: K2, KB19, inc 1. 23 sts total
Row 28: P3, PB18, P2
Row 29: K2, KB19, K2
Row 30: P2, PB20, inc 1. 24 sts total
Row 31: K2, KB21, inc 1. 25 sts total
Row 32: P2, PB22, inc 1. 26 sts total
Row 33: K3, KB21, K2
Row 34: P2, PB22, P2
Row 35: K2, KB23, inc 1. 27 sts total
Row 36: P3, PB22, P2
Row 37: K2, KB23, K2
Row 38: P2, PB24, inc 1. 28 sts total
Row 39: K3, KB23, K2
Row 40: P2, PB24, P2
Row 41: K2, KB25, inc 1. 29 sts total
Row 42: P3, PB24, P2
Row 43: K2, KB25, K2
Row 44: P2, PB26, inc 1. 30 sts total
Row 45: K3, KB25, K2
Row 46: P2, PB26, P2
Row 47: K2, KB27, inc 1. 31 sts total
Row 48: P3, PB26, P2
Row 49: K2, KB27, K2
Row 50: P2, PB28, inc 1. 32 sts total
Row 51: K3, KB27, K2
Row 52: P2, PB28, P2
Row 53: K2, KB29, inc 1. 33 sts total
Row 54: P3, PB28, P2
Row 55: K2, KB29, K2
Row 56: P2, PB30, inc 1. 34 sts total
Row 57: K3, KB29, K2
Row 58: P2, PB30, P2
Row 59: K3, KB29, K2
Row 60: P2, PB30, P2
Row 61: K2, KB31, inc 1. 35 sts total
Row 62: P3, PB30, P2
Row 63: K3, KB29, K1, K2tog. 34 sts total
Row 64: P3, PB28, P1, P2tog. 33 sts total

Row 65: K2, KB29, K2
Row 66: P3, PB28, P2
Row 67: K3, KB27, K1, K2tog. 32 sts total
Row 68: P2tog, P1, PB26, P1, P2tog. 30 sts total
Row 69: K2tog, K1, KB25, K2. 29 sts total
Row 70: P2tog, P1, PB24, P2. 28 sts total
Row 71: K2tog, K1, KB23, K2. 27 sts total
Row 72: P2tog, P1, PB22, P2. 26 sts total
Row 73: K2tog, K1, KB21, K2. 25 sts total
Row 74: P2tog, P1, PB20, P2. 24 sts total
Row 75: K2tog, K1, KB19, K2. 23 sts total
Row 76: P2tog, P1, PB18, P2. 22 sts total
Row 77: K2tog, K1, KB17, K2. 21 sts total
Row 78: P2tog, P1, PB16, P2. 20 sts total
Row 79: K2tog, K1, KB15, K2. 19 sts total
Row 80: P2tog, P1, PB14, P2. 18 sts total
Row 81: K2tog, K1, KB13, K2. 17 sts total
Row 82: P2tog, P1, PB12, P2. 16 sts total
Row 83: K2tog, K1, KB11, K2. 15 sts total
Row 84: P2tog, P1, PB10, P2. 14 sts total
Row 85: k2tog, K1, KB9, K2. 13 sts total
Row 86: P2tog, P1, PB8, P2. 12 sts total
Row 87: K2tog, K1, KB7, K2. 11 sts total
Row 88: P2tog, P1, PB5, P1, P2tog. 9 sts total
Row 89: K2tog, K1, KB4, K2. 8 sts total
Row 90: P2tog, P1, PB3, P2. 7 sts total
Row 91: purl
Row 92: K2tog, K3, K2tog. 5 sts total
Cast off

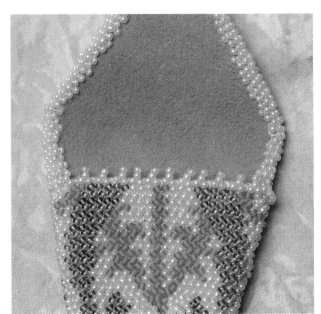

Front:

String the size 11 seed beads beginning at Row 52 on the design chart, and working down to Row 1, from either left to right or right to left (the design is symmetrical) onto the pearl cotton. Knit following the same directions as for the back through Row 52. Knit the next row. Purl the next row. Cast off.

Finishing:

1. Align the front and back, bead sides together, and stitch the seam close to the beads so there is no gap in the beads at the seam. Turn right side out.

2. Trace and then cut the front and back lining from leather (**Figure 9-2**). With right sides together, hand stitch together with a running stitch and using a leather needle, then stitch back the other way, filling in the spaces left from the first pass of running stitches (**Figure 9-3**).

3. Slip the suede lining inside of the bead knitting. To attach the flap to the leather and encase the edge with beads, anchor the beading thread at the base of the flap. Using the beading needle, string three to five beads and overcast stitch through the leather and the knitted selvage, covering the edge

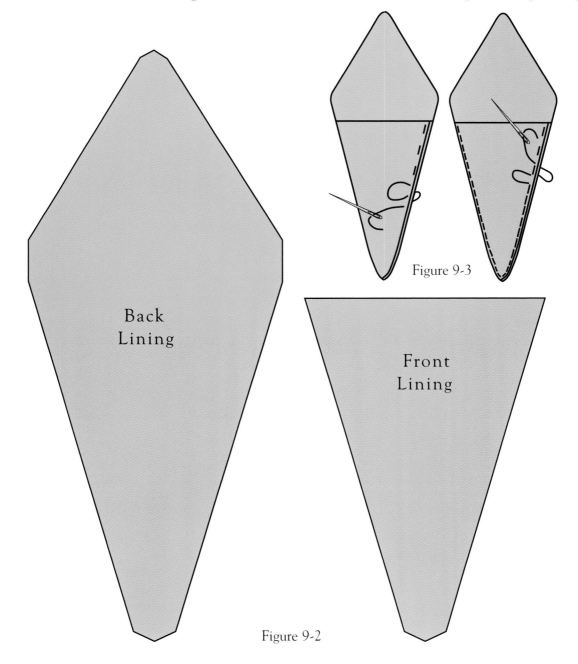

Figure 9-3

Back Lining

Front Lining

Figure 9-2

of the leather and the knitted selvage with beads. There should be no gap between the knitted beads and the beads on the overcast stitches (**Figure 9-4**).

4. Using the leather needle and pearl cotton, overcast stitch the front of the bead knitting to the edge of the leather (**Figure 9-5**).

5. Using the beading needle and beading thread, make a picot edge as shown in **Figure 9-6** at the top of the front, stitching in and out along the top row of beads in the knitting.

Closure:

1. Using the beading needle and beading thread, make two or three loops of seed bead strands on the front, just big enough so the large oval bead can slip through. Stitch several times through the leather and beads for a strong closure.

2. Using the beading needle and beading thread, sew the large oval bead to the point of the flap, stitching through the leather and creating a neck of seed beads long enough so the oval bead can be tilted to slide through the loop on the front (**Figure 9-7**).

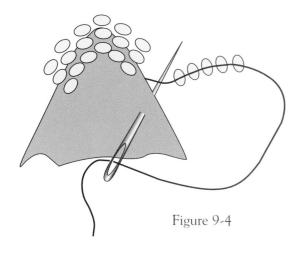

Figure 9-4

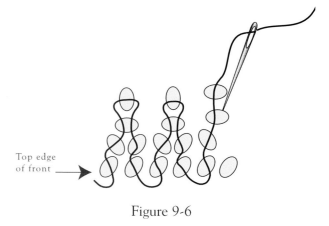

Top edge of front →

Figure 9-6

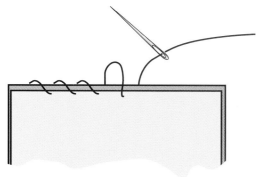

Figure 9-5

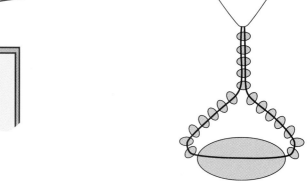

Figure 9-7

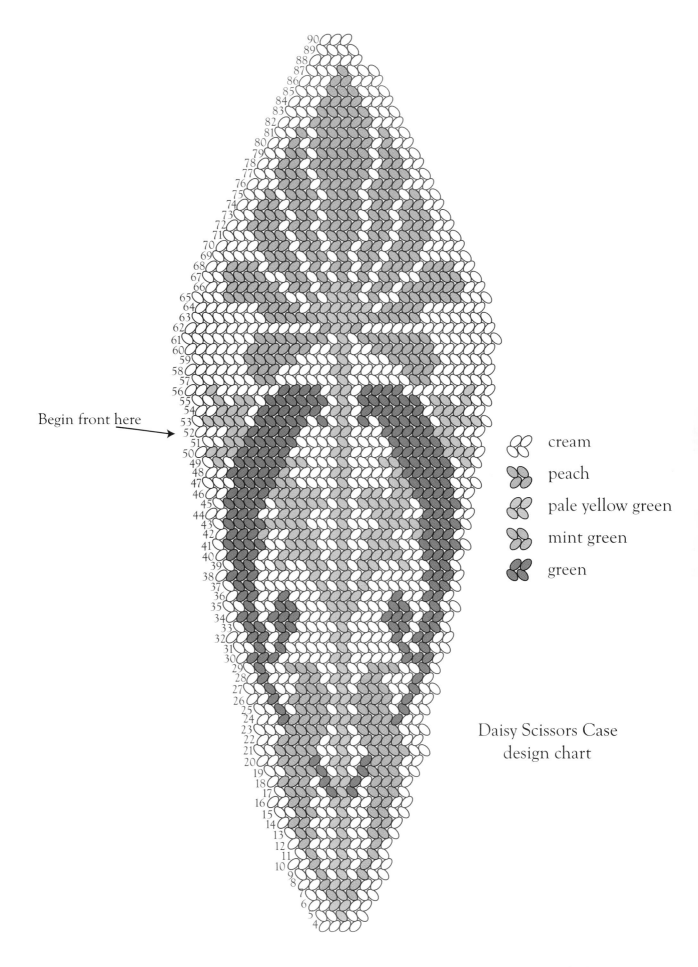

Begin front here →

90
89
88
87
86
85
84
83
82
81
80
79
78
77
76
75
74
73
72
71
70
69
68
67
66
65
64
63
62
61
60
59
58
57
56
55
54
53
52
51
50
49
48
47
46
45
44
43
42
41
40
39
38
37
36
35
34
33
32
31
30
29
28
27
26
25
24
23
22
21
20
19
18
17
16
15
14
13
12
11
10
9
8
7
6
5
4

cream

peach

pale yellow green

mint green

green

Daisy Scissors Case
design chart

Chapter 10
Crochet

This chapter teaches you two methods of using beads in single crochet:

• Bead crochet in the round with the beads in the back of the work.

• Flat bead single crochet with the beads in the front of the work. On alternate rows you work beads into the back of the work to keep the beads all on the same side.

Traditionally, bead crocheted projects were almost always crocheted in the round. It is easy to slide beads into the back of single crochet stitches, so the back side of the work becomes the beaded front of the finished piece.

Several bead crocheters have recently developed techniques for pulling the beads to the front of a crochet stitch so that we can now bead crochet on a flat piece, crocheting rows back and forth and always keeping the beads on the same side.

Before these developments, crocheters broke the thread at the end of each row and started a new one, beginning each row at the same side in order to stitch a flat beaded piece. I use the method developed by Elizabeth Gourley, one of my co-authors for the book *Art of Seed Beading*, for crocheting beads to the front of the stitch. When sliding a bead into the back of a stitch, the beads slant to the left if the bead is added at the beginning of the stitch, and they slant to the right if the bead is added after the stitch is started.

I like adding the beads at the beginning of the stitch for a consistent leftward slant in both flat and round beaded crochet. In flat front bead crochet, the beads also slant to the left in the method I use.

This flapper bag from the 1920s is crocheted and fabric-lined.

These are antique and contemporary bead crochet projects. The best way to find out which crochet technique was used is to look at a piece's back.

To make a beaded single crochet (BC):

1. Slide the hook into the stitch.

2. Slide a bead down to the work.

3. Thread around the hook clockwise.

4. Pull the thread through the stitch. The bead is in the stitch on the back of the work.

5. Thread around the hook clockwise.

6. Pull the thread through both loops on the hook.

7. The bead lies on the back side of the work. It will slant to the left.

To make a front beaded single crochet (FBC):

1. Slide the hook into the stitch.

2. Wrap the thread around the hook clockwise.

3. Pull the thread through the stitch, sliding a bead down to the hook and pushing the bead through the stitch as well, so it comes to the front.

4. Wrap the thread around the hook clockwise.

5. Pull the thread through both loops on the hook.

Abbreviations for this chapter
SC: single crochet
BC: single crochet with a bead in the back of the stitch
FBC: single crochet with a bead in the front of the stitch
CD: double crochet
st(s): stitch(es)
ch: chain

Bead Crocheted Star Sample

You Will Need

252 size 11 cream seed beads
Size 20 light blue DMC pearl cotton or

Cebelia
Size 8 crochet hook

This example teaches you how to slide the bead in place at the beginning of the stitch so the bead sits on the back of the stitch. You may want to practice in size 6 beads, using a sport-weight yarn and size H hook first, then try it with the smaller beads, thread, and hook once you get used to working with the beads.

Finished size: 2-1/4 inches in diameter

String 252 beads onto the thread (see page 71 in the knitting section).
Chain 3. Join into a ring.
Round 1: 7 SC in ring. 7 stitches.
Next you begin the continuous spiral rounds.
Round 2: BC and SC into the next stitch. Repeat around. 14 stitches.

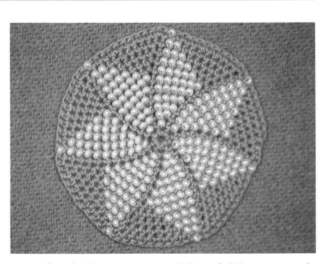

Round 3: (BC into next st, BC and SC in next st) x 7. 21 stitches.
Rounds 4 through 6: BC into each beaded stitch.

BC and SC in each stitch without a bead. Each round will increase by 7 stitches.

Make the points of the star:
Round 7: (BC into the next 5 sts, sc in next st, 2 sc in next st) x 7. 56 stitches.
Rounds 8 through 12: (BC 1 less than the round before and 1 more sc, then 2 sc in last st) x 7. The last round has no beads and 91 stitches.

Front Beaded Flat Crochet Sample

You Will Need

144 Size 11 seed beads
Size 8 DMC pearl cotton or size 20 Cebelia

Size 8 crochet hook

This sample teaches you how to make a flat front beaded single crochet panel. You may want to practice in size 6 beads, using a sport-weight yarn and size H hook first, then try it with the smaller beads, thread, and hook once you get used to working with the beads.

Finished size: 1-1/4 inches x 2-1/4 inches

String the beads onto the thread.
Ch 20.
Row 1: Ch1, SC in each chain, turn.
Row 2: Ch1, SC in each st, turn.
Row 3: Ch1, SC in first st, BC in each st to the

last st. SC in last st, turn.
Row 4: Ch1, SC in first st, FBC in each st to the last st. SC in last st, turn.
Rows 5-10: alternate Row 2 and Row 3.
Row 11 and 12: SC in each st. End.

Ocean Waves Bead Crochet Bag

You Will Need

1 ball size 20 Manuela blue variegated cotton crochet cord
60 grams size 11 clear glass Japanese seed beads
1 yard 1/8-inch cord for drawstring
2 small shells, with one drilled hole to fit a sewing needle

2 large shells with two drilled holes to fit the cord
Blue sewing thread and needle
Size 8 crochet hook
Clear craft glue for stabilizing the drawstring's cut ends

This is an easy beaded bag for avid thread crocheters. The fun closure with small shells to open the bag, and large shells to close it, add to the ocean theme of the wave pattern. I chose blue variegated thread with the colors aligning in a swaying pattern, showing through the clear glass beads. The closure idea is from a bag one of my students, Sherry Adkins, brought to class one day.

This bag is worked in continuously spiraling rounds. You may find it helpful to mark the beginnings of the rounds with a knit marker or a small safety pin while making the increases.

Finished size: 8 inches high by 11-1/2 inches around

To crochet the bag bottom and the side up to the wave pattern:
Slide 20 grams of beads onto the cotton crochet cord (see page 71).
Using a size 8 crochet hook, chain 3. Join into a ring.
Round 1: 7 SC in ring.
Round 2: BC and SC into the next st. Repeat around. 14 stitches.
Round 3: (BC into next st, BC and SC in next st) x 7. 21 stitches.
Round 4: BC into each beaded st. BC and SC in each st without a bead.
Continue as in Round 4 until there are 17 beads

and 1 SC without a bead, 7x around the edge. 126 stitches.

BC without increasing in every st. You are now crocheting the side of the bag. Continue until the bag measures 4-1/2 inches from the center bottom up to the working edge.

To crochet the sides with the wave design:

Begin following the Wave design chart, from right to left, bottom to top, making a SC for each blank square and a BC for each blue square. The beaded design will be reversed from the chart. Repeat the design chart 7x for each round of the bag.

SC in all stitches until the bag is 2 inches taller than the bead crochet waves.

To make the drawstring cord casing and shell stitch edging:

Reverse direction, so that the right side of the bag is facing you.

Row 1: Ch 3. DC in the next 2 sts. ch 1. (DC in the next 3 sts. ch 1) x 31, increasing 2 sts evenly around the bag. Slip stitch in third ch at beginning of the row. 128 sts.

Row 2: Ch 3. (DC in each DC, ch 1) x 32. 128 sts.

Rows 3 and 4: Ch 1, then SC in every st. Slip stitch in ch at beginning of the row. 128 sts.

Row 5: (7 treble crochet in fourth ch. Slip stitch in eighth ch.) x 16. End.

To add the drawstrings:

1. Apply glue to a 1/2-inch section of the center and ends of the drawstring cord to prevent raveling. When dry, cut the cord in half (for two 18-inch lengths).

2. Weave one length of cord through the openings in the bottom double crochet row and the other length of cord through the top double crochet row so that the cord tails meet at opposite ends of the rows (**Figure 10-1**).

3. Using sewing thread and a needle, stitch a small shell to the center of each cord and through to the double crochet, anchoring the cord to the bag at that point. These are now handles for opening the bag.

4. Thread the tail cords through the large shells and tie a square knot above the shell, so that the cords extend at least 1 inch beyond the bag when it is fully open.

5. Tie a knot in each tail close to the square knot. Cut the tails 1 inch from the knot and unravel to make a fringe. Cut the fringe evenly to about 3/4 inch.

Figure 10-1

Wave
design chart

Floral Belt Bag

You Will Need

1 tan-colored ball of size 10 DMC Cebelia
Size 8 seed beads in the colors shown in
    the Belt Bag design chart
1/2 oz. or 14 grams size 8 tan or brown seed
    beads for back of design
63 size 8 seed beads for flap
20 grams of size 15 green seed beads for flap
    edge

1 large accent bead
Various fringe beads to make a fringe of 21
    dangles (see Figure 10-2)
Size 5 crochet hook
Size 12 beading needle and thread
Chenille needle to weave in ends of crochet
    cotton

This small belt bag is a composite of ideas from two sources that inspired me: the beautiful brown bag on page 42 by Shonna Neuhart and the pattern on the antique purse on the title page. I used size 8 beads and a crochet technique in adapting these ideas to my belt bag. When crocheting in the round, the rows slant somewhat. To counteract this for this bag, crochet loosely and block the bag before adding the fringe.

Finished size: 2-1/4 inches x 5-1/4 inches, including fringe

String the 63 green size 8 beads for the flap. Then, string the pattern as shown in the Belt Bag design chart onto the cotton, following the pattern from right to left, top to bottom for each row. See page 71 for stringing instructions.

To make the bag:

1. Chain 44. Join into a ring with a slip stitch.

2. BC into each chain. 44 sts.

3. Continue BC spiraling around the bag, until all of the beads are crocheted.

To make the flap:

1. Reverse direction. Ch 1. SC in next 20 sts. Turn.

2. Ch 1. Skip next st. FBC in next 18 sts. Skip next st. SC in next st. Turn. 20 sts.

3. Ch 1. Skip next st. BC in next 16 sts. Skip next st. SC in last st. Turn. 18 sts.

4. Ch 1. Skip next st. FBC in next 15 sts. SC in last st. Turn. 17 sts.

5. Ch 1. Skip next st. BC in next 14 sts. SC in last st. End.

With the sewing thread and beading needle, stitch strands of size 15 seed beads along the edge of the flap as for the Knitted Scissors Case flap (on page 84). Sew the large accent bead in place.

To block the bag:
Wet the bag with water and pat off any excess with a towel. Shape the bag so it lies in a rectangle. Place a dishtowel on a cookie sheet and put the bag on it. Heat up your oven to 200 degrees. Place the cookie sheet with the beadwork in the oven and turn it off. This will set the shape of the bag with heat and water. Let the bag dry overnight.

To make the fringe:
Sew the bottom of the bag together. Thread the beading needle and alternate Fringe A and Fringe B with suggested beads across the bottom of the bag (**Figure 10-2**).

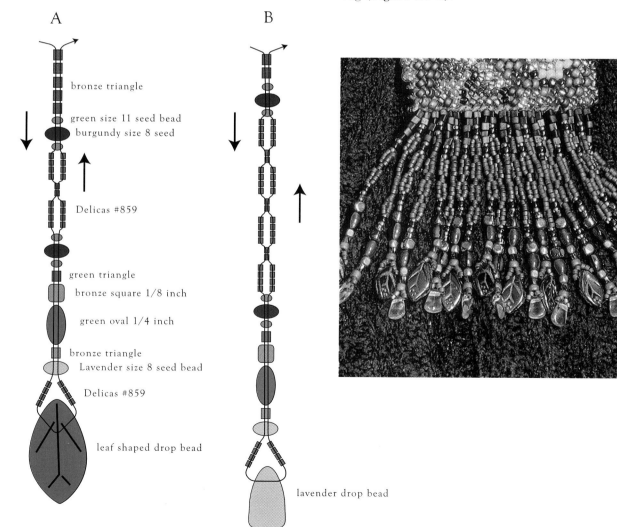

A

bronze triangle

green size 11 seed bead
burgundy size 8 seed

Delicas #859

green triangle
bronze square 1/8 inch

green oval 1/4 inch

bronze triangle
Lavender size 8 seed bead

Delicas #859

leaf shaped drop bead

B

lavender drop bead

Figure 10-2

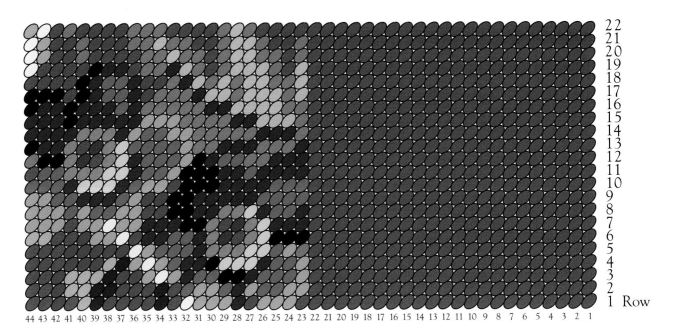

Bronze, 14 grams or 1/2 oz.

Small quantities needed of
the following colors

Black

Burgundy

Red

Rose

Pink

Brick

Gold

Yellow

Forest green

Green

Mint

Hunter green

Grass green

Pale green

Belt Bag
design chart

Purple Vine Crocheted Bracelet

_____ *You Will Need* _____

20 yards 1000 plum denier silk cord 2 spacer disks
6 grams size 15 plum seed beads   2 silver cones
2 grams size 15 lavender seed beads Size 10 crochet hook
2 large accent beads   Plum beading thread
Clasp   Size 12 beading needle
4 size 8 spacer beads

The firmness of this beaded rope comes from the number of beads in each round. The small beads, silk, and silver create an elegant design.

Finished size: 9 inches long

String the beads onto the silk, following the Crochet Bracelet design chart from right to left, top to bottom for each row. String Row 7 through Row 9, 43 more times. String Row 1 through Row 4 again.

Leave a 15-inch tail at the beginning for adding the accent beads.

1. Chain 12, putting a bead into each chain (**Figure 10-3**).

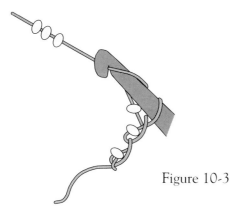

Figure 10-3

Tip: The first round of bead crochet tubes is very difficult because it is easy to lose track of which stitches to put your hook through. If you thread the first and last st in the beginning chain, each with a 3-inch length of contrasting thread and also the first st you make to join the chain into a loop, you will easily be able to know which stitch is which.

2. Slide the hook under the thread of the first chain stitch with a bead, to the left of the bead (**Figure 10-4**).

3. Slide a bead down to the hook, wrap the thread around the hook clockwise, and pull through both threads on the hook (**Figure 10-5**).

4. Repeat Steps 2 and 3, spiraling around, making a beaded slip stitch in every st, until all of the beads are crocheted. End.

5. Sew the cones, beads, and clasp. Using the tail thread, string the beads as shown in **Figure 10-6**. Pass through the clasp at the back and through the beads. Repeat and anchor into the crochet work; weave in all. Repeat for the other end of the bracelet, adding the other end of the clasp.

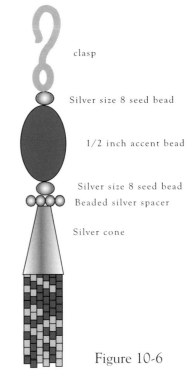

clasp

Silver size 8 seed bead

1/2 inch accent bead

Silver size 8 seed bead
Beaded silver spacer

Silver cone

Figure 10-6

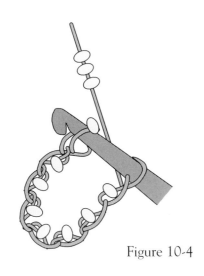

Figure 10-4

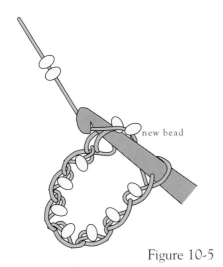

new bead

Figure 10-5

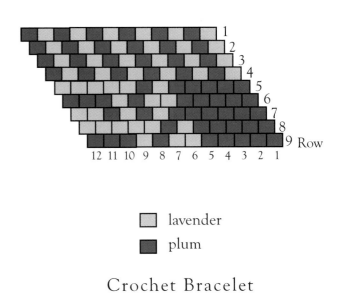

1
2
3
4
5
6
7
8
9 Row
12 11 10 9 8 7 6 5 4 3 2 1

☐ lavender
■ plum

Crochet Bracelet
design chart

Chapter 11
Tatting

The easiest way of incorporating beads into tatting is to string one type and color of bead onto the tatting thread and then slide them into all of the pattern's picots. This has the added advantage of providing uniform picots for beginning tatters. All picots end up the correct size, based on the number of beads used.

Unjoined picots look best with an odd number of beads so there is a point at the center of the picot. Picots that you join to other design elements can have an odd or even number of beads depending on the effect you want. The photograph below shows some of these possibilities.

You can use either needle or shuttle tatting with most patterns. Shuttle tatting limits you to using beads small enough to fit on the bobbin for tatting from the bobbin. You can get around this by stringing larger beads onto the ball and tatting off of the ball instead. Needle tatting has the advantage of letting you add larger beads onto the needle while tatting. (You will use both techniques in this book.)

I prefer tatting with beads close in size and color to the cord. I also like to incorporate plain picots with beaded picots to keep the delicate look of tatting.

You Will Need

Size 20 cream DMC Cebelia cotton cord
Tatting needle or shuttle

137 size 11 cream seed beads
Size 11 beading needle

Finished size: 2-1/4 inches by 5/8 inch

To make a sample of beaded needle tatting:

1. Thread the beading needle with the Cebelia and string all of the beads.

2. Remove the beading needle and thread the Cebelia onto the tatting needle and work from the ball.

3. Follow the diagram (**Figure 11-1**), sliding the number of beads as shown between chains instead of picots. Close the ring.

4. Slide nine beads up to the completed ring. This is the chain between rings.

5. Begin another ring, joining to the picot of the first ring. To join to a beaded picot, hold the tension tight on the thread, insert the needle into the picot so that there are two beads on either side, and pull the thread through, so that the loop of thread is between the two pairs of beads (**Figure 11-2**).

6. Finish the ring. Continue until there are six rings and five chains. Weave in the ends.

To make a sample of shuttle beaded tatting:

1. Thread the beading needle with the Cebelia and string all of the beads.

Sample made using size 30 cebelia and charlottes.

2. Remove the beading needle with the beaded Cebelia and wrap onto the bobbin.

3. Slide 18 beads into the ring.

4. Tat following the diagram in **Figure 11-1** to make the first ring, sliding the number of beads indicated into the picots.

5. Slide nine beads up to the completed ring. This is the chain between rings.

6. Make the next ring, joining to the first ring at the first picot. To join to a beaded picot, hold the tension tight on the thread, insert the hook or tip of the shuttle into the picot so that there are two beads on either side and pull the thread through, so that the loop of thread is between the two pairs of beads (**Figure 11-2**).

7. Continue until there are six rings and five chains. Weave in the ends.

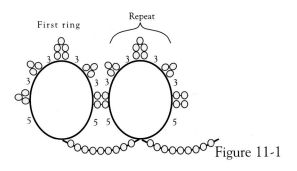

Figure 11-1

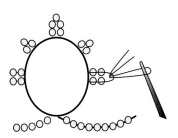

Figure 11-2

Needle Tatted Lampshade Fringe

You Will Need

Small table lamp with a shade 6 inches in
    diameter at the bottom opening
Size 20 dark blue Manuela cotton cord
Size #7 tatting needle
37 size 11 cobalt blue seed beads
37 small cobalt blue dagger drop beads

74 small cobalt blue drop beads
4 grams or 1/8 oz. size 15 cobalt blue seed
    beads
Size 11 beading needle
Tacky glue

Blue and white is my mother's favorite color combination. So this little lamp, with its blue and white color scheme, is perfect for decorating her new home.

Finished size: Will fit around a shade 6 inches in diameter at the bottom.

1. Thread the beading needle with the Manuela cotton; do not cut it from the ball.

2. String 37 repeats of the bead pattern (**Figure 11-3**). Change to the tatting needle.

3. Tat the pattern (**Figure 11-4**).

4. Weave the ends together to form a circle.

5. Pin to the lampshade, then carefully glue in place. When the glue is dry, remove the pins.

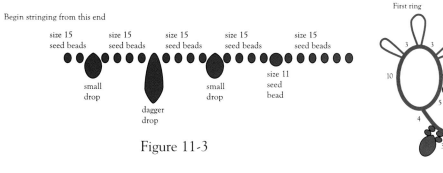

Begin stringing from this end

size 15 seed beads · size 15 seed beads · size 15 seed beads · size 15 seed beads · size 15 seed beads

small drop

dagger drop

small drop

size 11 seed bead

Figure 11-3

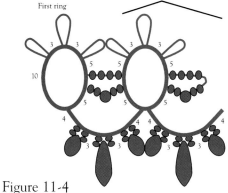

Repeat

First ring

Figure 11-4

Needle Tatted Mirror Case

You Will Need

2-3/4-inch pocket mirror with an opening on the back for inserting needlework
Tan-colored tatting thread
3-inch circle of sage-colored linen
155 size 15 cream-colored seed beads

10 cream-colored Delica beads
5 size 8 matte silver-lined gold beads
Size 7 tatting needle
Tan sewing thread and needle

This is a good example of the advantage of needle tatting with beads over shuttle tatting. Here, you have a needle to add beads as you work.

Finished size: 2 inches of tatting on a 2-3/4-inch mirror back.

1. Make one ring following **Figure 11-5**.

2. Close the ring.

3. Slide four beads up to the ring and string one Delica, one size 8 bead, and one Delica, then make another ring joining to the first (**Figure 11-6**).

4. Make a total of five rings, joining the last to the first. Weave in the ends.

5. Begin a new thread at one of the four bead picots on the ring. Following **Figure 11-7**, make the large chain, adding plain picots and beaded picots as shown. Repeat around the first round, attaching at each of the four remaining bead picots. Attach to the beginning picot and weave in the ends.

6. Sew the tatted piece to the linen, taking care to form the shape evenly. Insert the linen into the mirror back following the manufacturer's instructions.

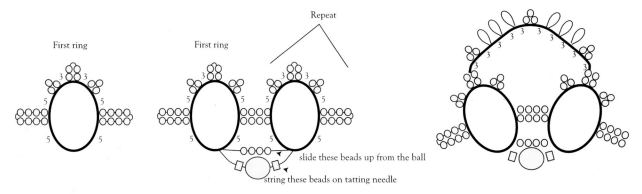

Figure 11-5   Figure 11-6   Figure 11-7

Shuttle Tatted Pin Cushion

You Will Need

Sudberry House Etcetera Pincushion #15761
10-inch circle of hunter green cotton
    velveteen
260 size 12 cream-colored charlottes
234 sea green-colored size 15 seed beads
26 gold charlottes

Cream-colored tatting thread
Tatting shuttle
Cream-colored sewing thread and needle
Large blunt needle
Size 12 beading needle
Sewing needle

Although you can also make this pattern with needle tatting, shuttle tatting creates a tighter stitch, making it easier to weave the second tatted section into the first.

Finished size: 4-inch circle of tatting on a 3-3/4-inch wide by 3/4-inch thick pin cushion, not including the wood base

To make the first row:
Using the beading needle, string the cream-colored charlottes onto the tatting thread.
Make 26 repeats of **Figure 11-8**, joining the last to the first, creating a circle.
Cut from the ball and weave in the ends.

To make the second row:
Using the beading needle, string 26 repeats of one gold charlotte and nine of the green beads onto the tatting thread. Make 26 repeats of **Figure 11-9**. Do not join into a circle. Cut from the shuttle, leaving a 6-inch tail.

To assemble the pin cushion:
1. Cover the pincushion with the velveteen, following the manufacturer's instructions. Pull the fabric only tight enough so the cushion is about 3/4 inch thick.

2. Pin the first row of tatting on the velveteen and stitch in place, going through only the picots and closing point of the rings.

3. Thread the large blunt needle with the tail of the second row of tatting and weave through the first row of tatting as in the project photo.

4. Use the sewing needle to hide the tails in the tatting.

5. Stitch the second row of tatting to the velveteen at the gold-beaded picots.

6. Follow the manufacturer's instructions for gluing the pincushion to the wood base.

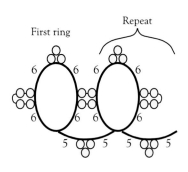

Figure 11-8

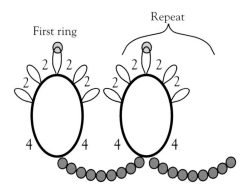

Figure 11-9

Chapter 12
Tambourwork

Tambour embroidery is the process of chain stitching with a tambour needle on fabric pulled tight in an embroidery hoop. The tambour needle is a hook similar to a crochet hook with a point at the tip to pierce the fabric. Different colored threads are used to make decorative chain stitches across the surface of the fabric. The hoop needs to be in a stand, because you need both hands free: one to hold the tambour needle on the topside of the hoop and the other to guide the thread on the underside.

When doing tambour embroidery with beads, the chain stitch is merely functional, and the beads carried on the thread on the right side of the fabric are the decorative feature.

Use a thin thread that blends with the color of the fabric so you can work the beads close together. A soft fabric such as velvet makes it easy to make the chain stitches.

The design for the tambourwork is drawn on the backside of the fabric which is stretched in the

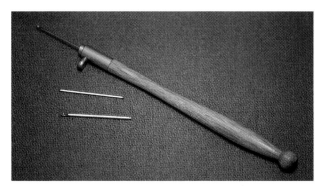

Tambour needles and handle.

hoop with the right side of the fabric facing down. Each bead is slid up to the fabric and caught in the underside of the chain stitch as it is made on the top of the fabric. The technique is simple, but practice is important so that the stitches are uniform. Each stitch should be just a little bit longer than the length of the bead you are using; hence stitch length varies according to the bead size.

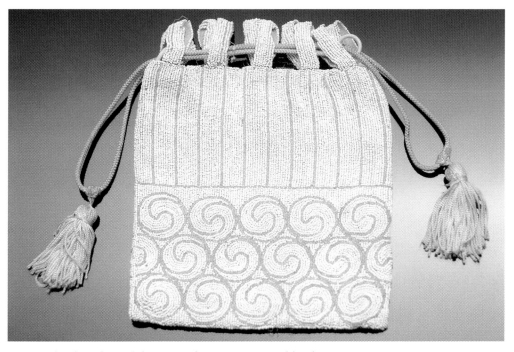

Antique bead tamboured drawstring bag in size 16 seed beads.

You Will Need

14-inch square of muslin
12-inch embroidery hoop and stand
Tambour needle size 90
DMC tatting thread size 80

Size 11 green seed beads
Tracing paper, transfer paper, and pencil
Size 11 beading needle
Size 10 crochet hook

Finished size: 2 inches by 3 inches

1. Transfer the design in the Tambourwork Sample design chart onto the back of the muslin with the tracing paper, transfer paper, and pencil. Stretch in the embroidery hoop with the design facing up. Put in the stand.

2. String about 15 inches of beads onto the tatting thread, keeping the thread on the ball. Insert the tambour needle in the tambour handle so that the hook faces the screw. Screw tight.

3. Holding the needle in your dominant hand, push it through the fabric at the beginning of the stem line.

4. With the other hand under the hoop, hold the thread about 6 inches from the end and loop it around the needle hook. Pull the needle up through the fabric, keeping tension on the thread below, and sliding the needle away from the hook side (the screw shows where the hook side is), so it glides back through without catching on the fabric. You should have pulled a loop up to the top side of the fabric (**Figure 12-1**).

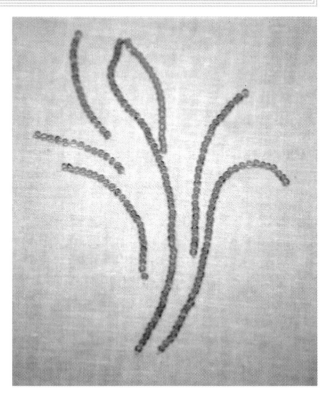

5. Pull the thread tail through to the top. Make a second stitch without a bead, close to the first. Thread the tail through the loop and pull tight to anchor the thread.

To add beads to the stitches:

1. Slide about 10 beads up the thread so that they are between your hand and the fabric. Practice moving one bead at a time up to the fabric without seeing what you are doing. You can also position a mirror below the work to see what you are doing, keeping in mind it will be a reverse image.

2. When you are comfortable sliding the beads, slide one bead up to the fabric and insert the tambour hook into the fabric about one bead's width away from the last stitch. Holding your hand

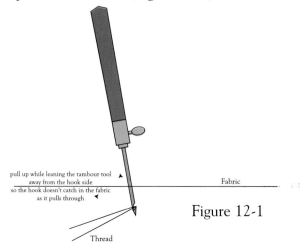

pull up while leaning the tambour tool
away from the hook side
so the hook doesn't catch in the fabric
as it pulls through

Fabric

Thread

Figure 12-1

under the hoop (**Figure 12-2**), guide the thread onto the hook and finish the stitch, catching the bead in the stitch.

3. Continue stitching with beads until you reach the end of the design. Take a small stitch without a bead and pull a loop of thread up to the back of the fabric.

4. Cut the thread, leaving about a 6-inch tail. Using the size 10 crochet hook, weave the tail through about five loops on the fabric to anchor it. Cut close to the fabric. Repeat for the beginning thread.

5. Repeat the process for each line of the design.

begin here

Tambourwork Sample
desing chart

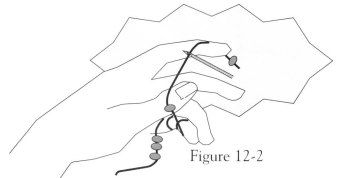

Figure 12-2

Bead Tamboured Needle Tool Box

You Will Need

Sudberry House Needle Tool Box #1595C
#90 Tambour needle and handle
8-inch embroidery hoop and stand
DMC tatting thread size 80

Size 11 blue, green, and turquoise seed beads
Size 11 beading needle
Tracing paper, transfer paper, pencil

Tambour embroidery is more fun when each color is a long, continuous line. That way, you tambour more and begin and end less. This small, easy project is a fun one to make. The thick pile of the velveteen hides the chain stitches and accents the beads nicely, giving the project an elegant look.

Finished size: 1-5/8-inch by 3-1/2-inch beaded area

1. Transfer the design in the Needle Tool Box design chart onto the back of the velveteen, using the tracing paper, transfer paper, and pencil.

2. Stretch the fabric, design side up, into a free-standing needlework frame.

3. String about 4 inches of one color beads onto the tatting thread, leaving the thread attached to the spool. Take the needle off of the thread.

4. Tambour embroider with beads along the first pattern line. End the thread and remove any excess beads.

5. Repeat Steps 3 and 4 for the other stitching lines, using different colored beads. Remove the fabric from the frame and follow the manufactur-er's instructions for inserting it into the needle tool box.

Needle Tool Box
design chart

Chapter 13

Needlepoint and Cross Stitch

Using beads in needlepoint and cross stitch projects adds texture and dimension to the design. The beads are easily added by making a half cross stitch, or tent stitch, with a bead picked up on the thread before completing the stitch.

You need to use a needle small enough to fit the bead hole and use beads that fill the stitch size of the evenweave fabric.

You can use beads sparingly as in the top of the Sampler shown on page 139, to accent the foreground design as in the Needlepoint Glasses Case on page 108, or throughout the piece as the antique beaded tray below. You can also add more dimension by using strands of beads across the surface.

Traditionally, beads are stitched using a neutral colored thread, but I like to match the thread to the bead colors to fill the space with the same color. Transparent beads are enhanced when you choose a thread color to match or brighten the hue.

Beaded purses and bags, such as this antique needlepoint drawstring floral bag, have gone in and out of style since the seventeenth century.

This beautiful antique serving tray was made using size 11 seed beads and gold-toned steel-cut beads, in needlepoint, on Penelope canvas.

Needlepoint Glasses Case

You Will Need

10 by 10 inches of 18-count Aida cloth
8- by 8-inch lining fabric
Needlework frame
Size 8 seed beads, in the colors shown in
    the Glasses Case design chart
Size 8 DMC pearl cotton to match beads (use
    royal blue background thread to stitch the

beads on the butterfly)
Two skeins of Impressions by Caron needle-
    work thread, 50% silk/50% wool, medium
    blue # 7044
2 feet of 1/4-inch dark blue cord
Size 22 and 26 needlepoint needles
Sewing thread and needle to match lining

I was inspired by a carved soapstone butterfly to create this case. I chose 18-count Aida cloth because it has the correct spacing to fit size 8 seed beads. First, I stitched the beads across two stitches with the Aida stretched on a frame. Then, I began the needlepoint stitches.

Work the leaf stitch and Florentine stitch on a frame using a laying tool to make the two strands of Impressions thread lie flat. You can work the other single-strand stitches in the hand without a frame.

Finished size: 7-1/4 by 4 inches

To stitch the design:

1. Following the Glasses Case design chart, stitch the beads with matching colors of pearl cotton and the size 22 needlepoint needle using the tent stitch.

2. Using two strands of Impressions, stitch the leaf stitch, Florentine stitch, and tent stitch sec-

tions, following the numerical sequence in the stitch diagrams (**Figures 13-1, 13-2, and 13-3**).

3. Stitch the fern stitch using a single strand of Impressions, following the diagram (**Figure 13-4**). Stitch the dark blue background in fern stitch, using the royal blue pearl cotton you used to stitch the butterfly beads on.

4. Stitch the running cross stitch variation using a single strand of Impressions, following the diagram (**Figure 13-5**).

To make the case:

1. Trim the raw edges of Aida cloth to 1/4 inch from the needlework. Turn under and press. Blind hem stitch the bottom and side edges together to make the glasses case.

2. Fold the lining fabric in half with right sides together. Stitch a 1/2-inch seam on the long side and one short side. Trim the seam to 1/4 inch and slip inside the glasses case.

3. Fold the raw edge of the lining over to line up with the top edge of the glasses case. Blind hem stitch in place.

4. Blind hem stitch the cord around the sides and bottom of the case and make a loop at the side and tie in a knot. Knot the tail and cut 1-1/2 inches from the knot. Unravel the cord up to the knot to make a fringe. Cut to 1 inch.

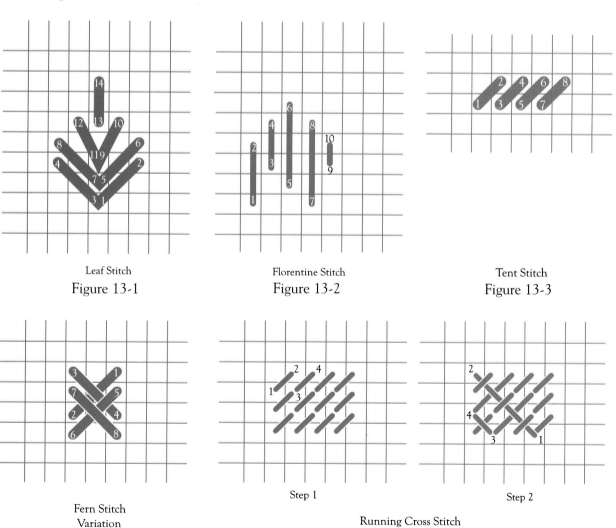

Leaf Stitch
Figure 13-1

Florentine Stitch
Figure 13-2

Tent Stitch
Figure 13-3

Fern Stitch
Variation
Figure 13-4

Step 1

Step 2

Running Cross Stitch
Variation

Figure 13-5

Leaf Stitch   Fern Stitch   Florentine Stitch   Running Cross Stitch

Impressions needlework yarn
Royal blue DMC pearl cotton
Green metallic beads
Matte purple beads
Lilac beads
Black beads
Dark blue beads
Lavender beads
Pink beads
Yellow beads
Clear beads

Glasses Case
design chart

Cross Stitch and Beads Business Card Holder

You Will Need

3- by 4-inch 14-count Aida cloth in a dark, neutral color

DMC six-strand floss:
815 dark red
820 royal blue
918 brown
3787 dark mushroom
712 cream
310 black

Size 11 seed beads to match each of the floss colors above

4- by 9-inch piece of dark red Ultra Suede

4- by 5-1/4-inch piece of dark blue Ultra Suede

Size 26 needlepoint needle

Size 10 bead embroidery needle

Size 12 sharps needle

Size B Nymo

Thimble

Heavy, double-sided fusible interfacing

This design was inspired by the beautiful rugs my mother's friend, Albert Desrosiers, collects. I was privileged to sit in on their weekly quartet gatherings, listening to live chamber music, in a home where the floors, walls, and tables were covered with outstanding Persian and oriental rugs, antique molas, stained glass windows, and brilliant cut glass. It was a wonderful, inspiring setting.

Finished size: 2-3/4 by 3-1/2 inches

To make the cross stitch and beadwork:

1. Using three strands of floss and no beads, cross stitch all of the dark red following the Business Card Holder design chart. Stitch the black border in the same way.

2. Stitch the rest of the design using beads and two strands of floss the same color as the beads. Make half cross stitches with beads, the same direction as the first half of the cross stitch used in Step 1.

3. Turn under the edges of the Aida cloth so only the stitching shows. Press.

To make the case:

1. Cut the interfacing 1/16 inch smaller than the beadwork. Press the beadwork onto the blue suede **(Figure 13-6)**.

Figure 13-6

2. Cut another piece of interfacing 1/16 inch smaller all around than the blue suede and another piece 1-3/4 by 3-3/4 inches. Stack **(Figure 13-7)**. Press in place.

3. Bead the edge design **(Figure 13-8)** and stitch all of the pieces together, using black beads, the beading thread, beading needle, and a thimble.

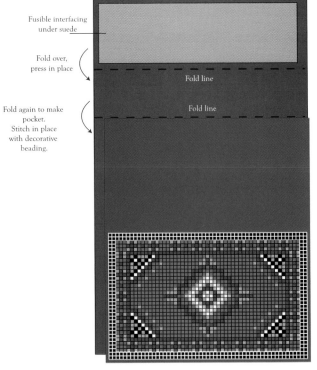

Fusible interfacing under suede

Fold over, press in place — Fold line

Fold again to make pocket. Stitch in place with decorative beading. — Fold line

Figure 13-7

Figure 13-8

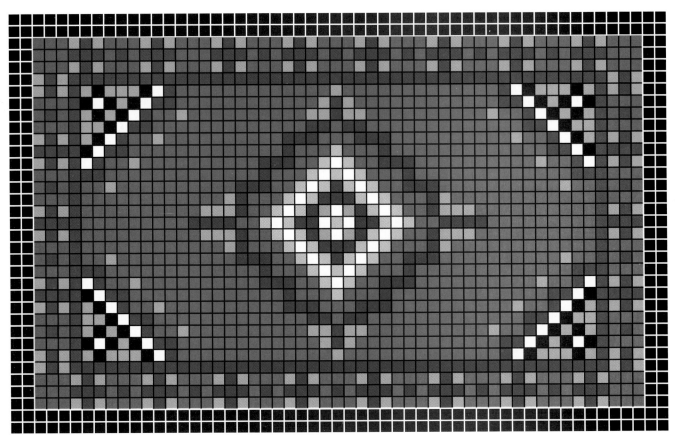

Business Card Holder
design chart

Chapter 14

Embroidery

Using beads in embroidery by stitching short strands of beads on fabric opens up a whole world of freedom in surface embellishment. The bead size and placement do not have to conform to a grid. And, if you find you need more color in an area you have completed, you can simply stitch on a few more beads; you don't have to undo rows of beadwork before you can make color or design changes.

Beaded edgings also give you a lot of creative freedom. You can use edgings to join two pieces of fabric while embellishing a piece. Edgings can be simple, like that shown on the Bead Embroidered Chatelaine (on page 117), or very elaborate, such as the fringe on the amulet bag by Delinda V. Amura on page 114. They can add greatly to the quality of the piece just by giving it a clean finish as in the Sage Jewelry Bag project on page 115.

Photo by Myra Nunley

This elegant bag, made by adding beads to a ribbon, was designed and beaded by Carole Tripp.

Embroidered butterfly on a velvet bag, designed and beaded by Delinda V. Amura.

Sage Jewelry Bag

You Will Need

One 6- by 4-inch and two 3-1/2- by 4-1/2-
    inch pieces of dusty green Ultra Suede
20 4mm round aventurine beads
Size 11 dark, medium, and light green seed
    beads, 3 grams or 1/8 oz. of each

40 size 8 green triangle beads
Frog closure
Beading thread to match suede
Size 11 beading needle
Paper clips

This easy beaded edging adds elegance to a simple project. All suede sections are double thickness for a sturdy bag. You stitch a beaded edging around the two front pieces and then join the beaded edging to the two back pieces. Then you bead the edges of the flap and attach a frog closure.

Finished size: 4 by 3 inches closed

1. Cut the front of the bag from the large piece of Ultra Suede folded in half, using **Figure 14-1** as a pattern and folding the suede along the fold on the pattern.

2. Use paper clips to hold the fold together.

3. Stitch the edging pattern (**Figure 14-2**) around the raw edges of the folded front, stitching through both front pieces to join them together.

4. Stitch the top edging (**Figure 14-3**), 1/8 inch from the fold.

5. Cut two of pattern **Figure 14-1** from Ultra Suede.

6. Paper clip the back and flap pieces as one to the front beaded piece. Stitch all around (**Figure 14-4**).

7. Stitch the frog closure parts to the flap and body of the bag.

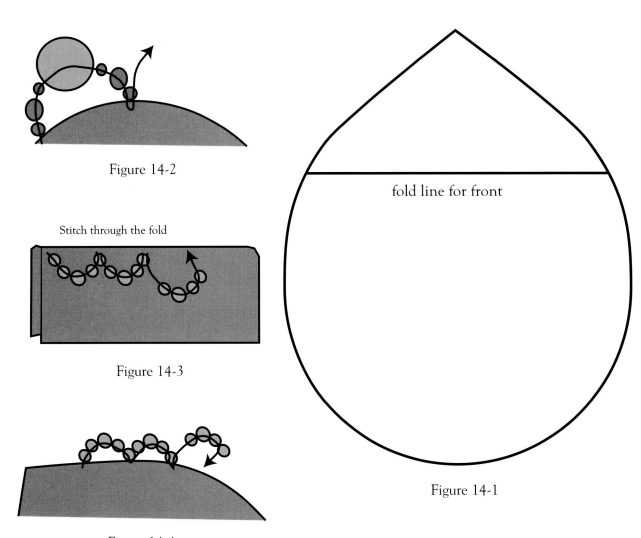

Figure 14-2

Stitch through the fold

Figure 14-3

fold line for front

Figure 14-1

Figure 14-4

Bead Embroidered Chatelaine

You Will Need

Two 4-1/2- by 2-1/4-inch pieces of emerald green Ultra Suede

5 grams or 1/4 oz. size 15 silver lined pale aqua seed beads

7 grams or 1/4 oz. size 11 aqua AB seed beads

Size 8 silver lined pale aqua triangle beads

Various accent beads for the neck chain and chatelaine edging (see Figure 14-9 for design ideas and to calculate the quantities needed)

Size 11 and 13 beading needles

Beading thread to match Ultra Suede

Paper clips

Tracing paper and pencil

This project combines beaded edgings, bead embroidery, and bead stringing to create an elegant accessory for a special pair of scissors.

Finished size: 3-3/4 by 2-1/4 inches, not including chain

To make the chatelaine:

1. Cut two of the pattern (**Figure 14-5**) from Ultra Suede.

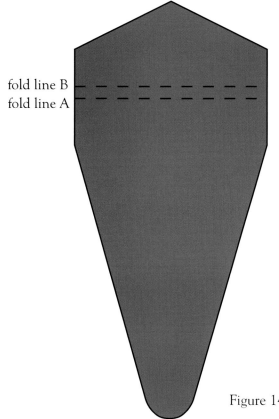

fold line B

fold line A

Figure 14-5

2. Trace the designs in **Figure 14-6**. Pin the top pattern to one side of one piece of Ultra Suede and the bottom pattern to the other side. Embroider through the tracing paper. Use back stitching for the vine and straight stitches for the leaves. Tear the tracing paper off.

3. Fold the beaded piece at fold line "A" as shown in **Figure 14-5** and the plain piece at fold line "B." Hold together with paper clips with the folds (wrong side) facing out.

4. Use size 11 beads and stitch the sides together following the pattern (**Figure 14-7**). Stitch the

beads closer together at the curve, adding the accent bead (**Figure 14-8**).

5. Use size 15 beads and stitch the same edging along the bottom of the flaps.

To make the neck chain:

1. Thread the needle with a doubled thread long enough to make a neck strap plus 12 inches for sewing the ends to the bag.

2. Attach to one side of the bag going through 1/2 inch of the Ultra Suede.

Stitch on the back side of the suede

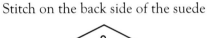

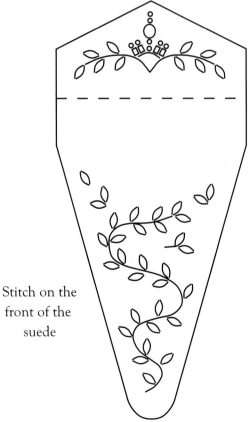

Stitch on the front of the suede

Figure 14-6

Figure 14-7

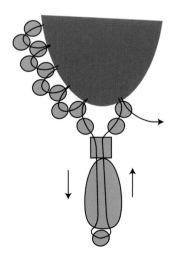

Figure 14-8

3. String the beads on the doubled thread in the suggested order (**Figure 14-9**).

4. Stitch down the second end of the neck chain about 1/2 inch through the Ultra Suede to attach it securely to the chatelaine.

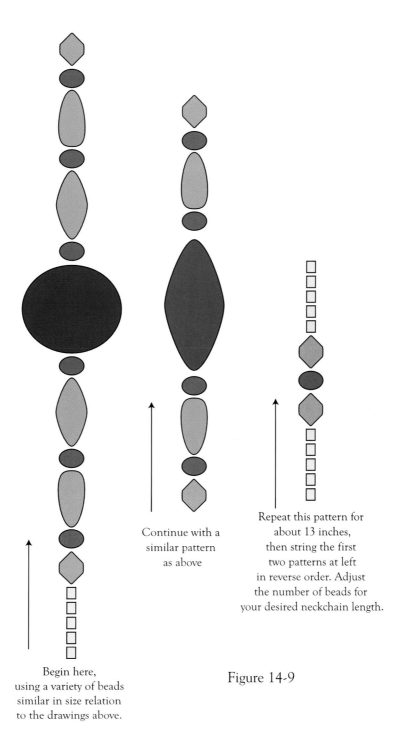

Begin here,
using a variety of beads
similar in size relation
to the drawings above.

Continue with a
similar pattern
as above

Repeat this pattern for
about 13 inches,
then string the first
two patterns at left
in reverse order. Adjust
the number of beads for
your desired neckchain length.

Figure 14-9

Chapter 15
Knotted Silk

Necklaces of strung beads separated by knots have always been the hallmark of fine jewelry. Originally, the knots were there to keep the expensive beads from falling to the ground should the thread break. They also protected the beads from the abrasion of rubbing against each other.

Silk or nylon cord with a wire needle is the preferred medium for stringing a bead-knotted necklace. Use the thickest cord that will fit through the smallest bead you plan to string. Specialty knotting tools are available just for making knotted bead necklaces, but a small-sized round nosed pliers will also hold the forming knot close to the bead for a nice, tight placement.

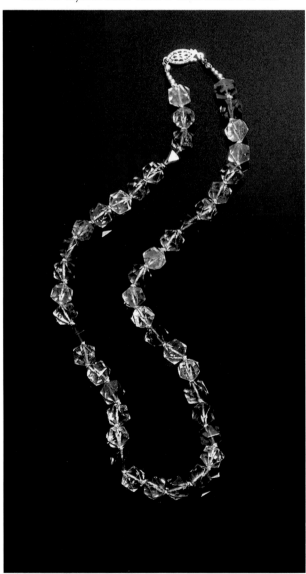

Faceted Fluorite bead-knotted necklace, designed and constructed by Cheryl Council.

Multi-strand freshwater pearl and glass bead necklace, designed and constructed by Cheryl Council.

Silk Beaded Knotted Necklace

To practice knotting, string some size 11 seed beads onto size 20 Cebelia and knot between each bead until you can get the knots close to each bead.

Finished size: 18 inches

1. Unwind the beading cord with the wire needle attached. Tie an overhand knot 1 inch from the end and string through one bead tip (**Figure 15-1**). Put a dab of glue on the knot. Let dry, then cut the tail close to the glued knot inside the bead tip.

2. Make another overhand knot on the outer side of the bead tip. Hold the cord with the round nosed pliers (**Figure 15-2**) so the knot will tighten next to the bead tip. This is how all the knots are made in this necklace.

3. String all of the beads onto the cord and tie a slipknot near the needle so the beads won't fall off. Push the first bead up to the knot next to the bead tip. Tie a knot as in Step 2, close to the bead. Try to make the knots with enough room for the bead so that the growing necklace hangs smoothly, but without any excess cord showing between the beads, only the knot.

4. Slide the next bead up toward the first, holding it next to the knot, and make another knot to

hold the new bead in place. Repeat until all of the beads are held between knots.

5. Pull out the slipknot near the needle and pick up the other bead tip and tie a knot inside the bead tip. Put a dab of glue on this knot and let dry. Cut the excess thread close to the glued knot. Let dry.

6. Slip a jump ring onto the hook of one of the bead tips and roll the hook into the bead tip with the needle nosed pliers. Repeat for the other bead tip.

7. Slide one side of the clasp onto each jump ring.

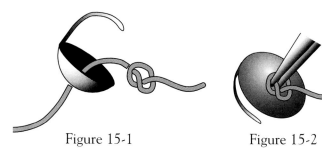

Figure 15-1   Figure 15-2

Chapter 16

Stranding

Stranding is a term I've chosen for techniques involving stringing strands of beads without knotting. The beads are strung into loops or strands and then twisted or woven to create three-dimensional effects. These techniques are quick ways to work with beads and create complex looking effects.

It is important to make the strands tight, so there are no gaps of thread, before twisting or weaving; otherwise, the thread will lock together between the beads as you try to pull one strand through another. Before weaving with a strand of beads, always pass through the last bead strung, pushing it up to the other beads so they are locked in place (**Figure 16-1**).

Many projects can be made by stringing large numbers of one type of bead. An easy technique I use for picking up five or more of the same bead is to pour a pile of beads on a mat and scoot the needle through the pile until it is almost filled, then slide the beads onto the thread in groups of five. This becomes a very quick process with practice.

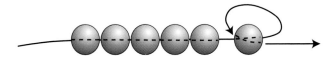

Figure 16-1

Beaded boxes from the book Beaded Boxes, *by Jane Davis.*

Blue and Copper Bracelet

You Will Need

20 grams or 3/4 oz. blue size 11 seed beads (A)
140 size 11 silver-lined brown seed beads (B)
12 oval 3/16-inch long copper beads (C)
26 rounded square 1/8-inch copper beads (D)
18 size 6 transparent brown beads (E)

36 carnelian chips (F)
2 round 1/4-inch beads (G)
Clasp
Size 11 beading needle
Size B black Nymo

This is a fun bracelet to make, with many possibilities for different looks if you change some of the beads. I have assigned letter codes to the types of beads in the materials list so you can easily change the design to suit your color preferences. The only consideration is that the beads at each end of the bracelet have holes large enough to allow at least 11 passes of the thread. I use one long strand of thread so I don't have to pass through the end beads more than necessary.

Finished size: 8 inches long.

Note: To adjust the size of this bracelet, add or subtract three of the (A) beads from each strand for each 1/4-inch adjustment.

1. Cut three yards of Nymo. Thread through the clasp and tie the ends in a square knot so that the clasp is in the middle of the thread.

2. Thread the needle with one of the thread ends. Pick up one bead (G) and one bead (D). String the following sequence of beads:
    a. 20 (A)
    b. 1 (B), 1 (C), 1 (B)
    c. 20 (A)
    d. 1 of each (B), (D), (B), (E), (B), (D), (B)
    e. 20 (A)
    f. 1 of each (B), (F), (B), (F), (B), (F), (B)
    g. 1 (E)
    h. 1 of each (B), (F), (B), (F), (B), (F), (B)

3. Repeat stringing e through a in reverse order.

4. Pick up one bead (D) and one bead (G). Pass through the other side of the clasp and back through beads (G) and (D). One strand is completed.

5. Repeat the stringing sequence in Steps 2 and 3. Pass through beads (D) and (G) and the clasp, then back through beads (D) and (G) again (**Figure 16-2**). Two strands are now completed.

6. Make four more strands as in Step 5, always passing through the two beads at the end, through the clasp, then back through the two beads at the

end again, ready to string more beads. Six strands are now completed. Knot the thread at the clasp and weave back into one of the strands for about 1-1/2 inches. Cut excess.

7. Thread the remaining tail and make two more strands only with bead (A), stringing on beads until the strand is the same length as the completed strands. Eight strands are now completed.

8. String a repeat of 10 of bead (A) and one of bead (B) until the strand measures the same as the other strands. Repeat. Ten strands are now completed.

9. Knot the thread and weave back into one of the strands for about 1-1/2 inches. The bracelet will be more than 9 inches long at this point, but will tighten up in the following steps.

10. Now split the strands into two sections, five on each side, and pass one end through the opening (**Figure 16-3**). Repeat three more times.

11. Make new openings by pulling two or three strands over to the other five-strand section. Pass one end of the bracelet through this opening (**Figure 16-4**). Repeat at the other end, and several times more, experimenting until you are happy with the shape of the bracelet.

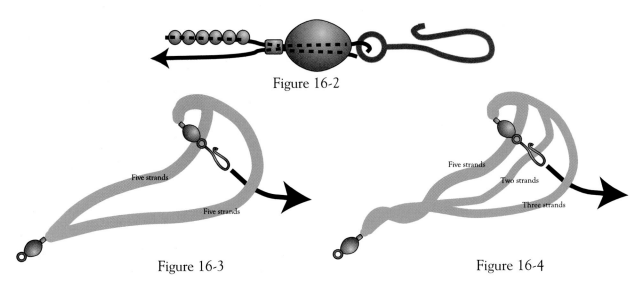

Figure 16-2

Five strands
Five strands

Figure 16-3

Five strands
Two strands
Three strands

Figure 16-4

Using the stranding idea and the same beads as the Blue and Copper Bracelet project on page 123, this necklace, by Jane Davis, was made with a Lampwork bead by Blue Heeler Glass as the centerpiece.

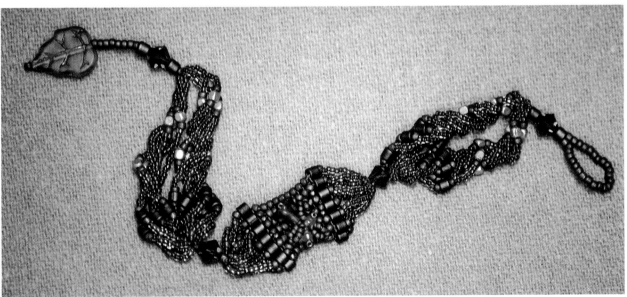

Forest Glen bracelet, designed and stitched by Jane Davis. A herringbone embellished centerpiece is flanked by twisted strands of beads to make this unusual bracelet.

Chapter 17
Wirework

To watch a skilled wire artist take a straight piece of wire and wind it into a beautiful work of art is an amazing thing, like watching a clown at the fair magically transform a few balloons into a poodle. It's one of those skills that needs quite a bit of practice because the wire needs to be bent into the desired shape the first time for a clean, smooth form.

There are several styles of wirework. Designs in wire can be carefully planned with a great deal of measuring, marking, and taping, or they can be free and wild, with little uniformity; however, most wirework takes planning, no matter how random it appears. Beads used in wirework need to have holes big enough for the wire to pass through. By combining different gauges of wire, a larger variety of beads can be added to a wirework project, without sacrificing strength in the piece's structure.

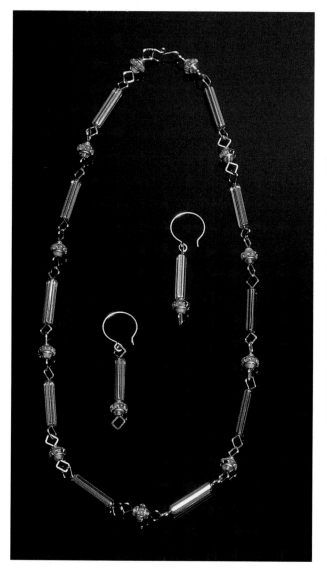

Wire and beads can be used for simple projects like these nifty key chains, by Kathy Henjyoji.

Wire and beads can also be used for elegant jewelry like this necklace and earrings, by Cheryl Council.

Wirework Beaded Bracelet

This bracelet is a good introduction to wire-work techniques. It helps if you practice wrapping the basic loops until you are comfortable with the technique before making the bracelet.

Finished size: 7-1/2 inches long

1. Cut a 2-1/2-inch piece of wire.

2. Grab the wire about 1 inch from one end with the round nosed pliers and bend to a 45-degree angle. Without letting go of the wire, take the flat nosed pliers and bend the 1-inch end tightly around the pliers, until you've made a loop with the excess wire sticking beyond the loop (**Figure 17-1**).

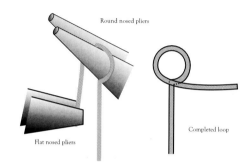

Figure 17-1

3. Because the round nosed pliers are tapered, the size of the loop will be determined by where you hold the wire on the pliers. Experiment until you like the loop size you make, then try to hold the wire at the same place every time. Don't make this first loop smaller than 1/8 inch because it is the loop part of the clasp.

4. Take the flat nosed pliers and hold the loop tightly. Wrap the 3/8-inch tail tightly around the straight wire three times with the round nosed pliers (**Figure 17-2**). Cut close to the wrap.

5. String one bronze size 11 bead, one pearl, and one bronze size 11 bead onto the wire.

6. Grab the wire with the round nosed pliers about 1/8 inch from the last bead, make a loop as described in Step 2, and wrap the tail around the wire as in Step 3, ending next to the beads. The first style of wire link is complete (**Figure 17-3**).

7. Repeat Steps 1 and 2 with another wire, then slide the first beaded wire section into the loop.

8. Repeat Step 4.

9. String one green size 11 bead, one bronze size 11 bead, one 6mm bead, one bronze size 11 bead, and one green size 11 bead onto the wire. Repeat Step 6. The second style of beaded wire link is complete.

10. Continue making the two styles of links, until there are ten completed beaded wire links, five of each kind.

11. The last link includes a hook. Cut a 4-inch piece of wire. Fold down 1-1/2 inches and pinch tight with the flat nosed pliers (**Figure 17-4**).

12. Grab the folded wire 3/4 inch from the fold with the flat nosed pliers and grab the small tail with the round nosed pliers. Wrap the small tail around the long tail three times. Cut excess (**Figure 17-5**).

13. Bend the folded section into the shape of a hook. This is the hook part of the clasp. Slide the same bead pattern as the first link made onto the long tail and make the loop, sliding the last link made into the loop to complete the bracelet.

14. To make a safety catch, make five more small links and attach them to the links as shown (**Figure 17-6**).

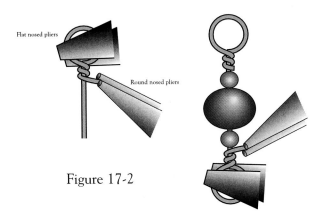

Figure 17-2

Figure 17-3

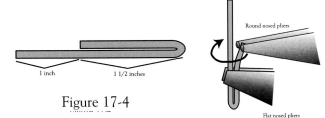

Figure 17-4

Figure 17-5

Figure 17-6

Beads and Wire Floral Detail

You Will Need

12 inches of 20-gauge wire
45 inches of 26-gauge wire
Small amounts of size 11 seed beads, three
    shades of green, three shades of purple, gold
Small amounts of green triangle beads or size
    8 seed beads

Size 15 green seed beads
Round nosed pliers
Flat nosed pliers
Size 11 beading needle
Green size B beading thread

Use this little ornament to decorate a special package, as a pin to wear, or as an accent on a wreath as shown in the photo below. The combination of wire and threadwork give the piece structure as well as the ability to increase beading detail.

Finished size: 3-inch long leaf and stem

To make the leaf:

1. Bend the 20-gauge wire (**Figure 17-7**), stringing the triangle or size 8 beads.

2. Cut an 8-foot length of beading thread and thread the needle. Tie the thread between the first and second bead on the center wire of the leaf (**Figure 17-8**).

3. Pick up one medium green size 11 seed bead and wrap around one of the leaf's side wires, between two large beads. Pass back through the size 11 bead (**Figure 17-9**).

4. Pick up another medium green bead and wrap around the center wire, between the second and third large bead. Pass back though the medium green bead (**Figure 17-10**).

5. Repeat Step 3. Now pick up three medium beads and wrap around the center wire, then pass back through the last bead strung (**Figure 17-11**).

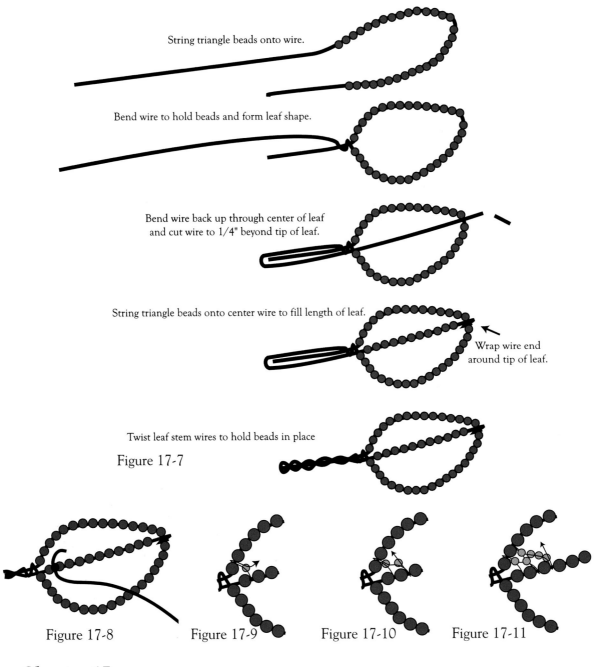

String triangle beads onto wire.

Bend wire to hold beads and form leaf shape.

Bend wire back up through center of leaf and cut wire to 1/4" beyond tip of leaf.

String triangle beads onto center wire to fill length of leaf.

Wrap wire end around tip of leaf.

Twist leaf stem wires to hold beads in place

Figure 17-7

Figure 17-8   Figure 17-9   Figure 17-10   Figure 17-11

6. Pick up three more beads, wrap around the side wire, and pass back through the last bead strung (**Figure 17-12**).

7. Repeat Step 6, stringing enough beads to fill the space between the two wires and each time passing around the wire between the next two beads along the wire. Choose bead colors to make the leaf show highlights and shadows. You will increase the number of beads in each pass to the widest point of the leaf, and then begin decreasing, until you get to the tip or end of the leaf. The strands of beads will be doubled across the leaf, one for the pass to the side of the leaf and one for the pass to the center of the leaf.

8. Repeat for the other side of the leaf, working back to the base of the leaf. Knot the thread and pass through several strands, then cut close to the beadwork. Repeat for the tail thread.

To cover the stem with beads:

1. Cut 12 inches of the 26-gauge wire and wrap one end tightly around the base of the leaf.

2. String 5 inches of the size 15 beads onto the 26-gauge wire and wrap it tightly around the stem (**Figure 17-13**).

3. Add or take off beads so there are just enough beads to cover the 20-gauge wire. Tuck the 26-gauge tail into the stem and cut the wire close to the beadwork.

To make the flowers:

1. Pick up three gold beads on the remaining 26-gauge wire and twist together (**Figure 17-14**), leaving a 3-inch tail.

2. Pick up 15 of one color of the purple beads and twist into a loop close to the gold beads (**Figure 17-15**).

3. Repeat Step 2 until there are seven or eight purple loops on the wire. Twist the beginning and ending wires (**Figure 17-16**). Arrange the purple loops around the gold beads to create a flower.

4. Make two more flowers, each about 1/2 inch apart, using a different color purple for each one. Wrap the wire around the stem of the leaf, positioning the flowers on one side of the leaf. Use the excess wire to attach the finished beadwork to a ribbon, bow, or pinback.

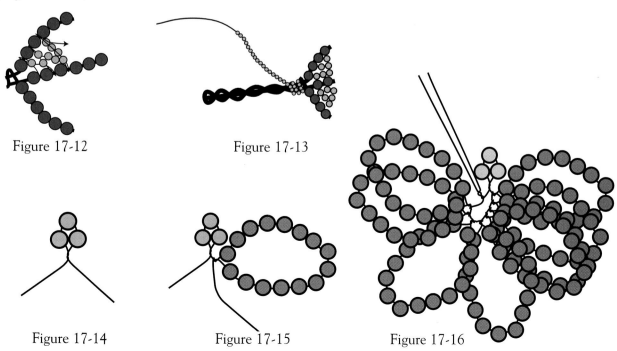

Figure 17-12

Figure 17-13

Figure 17-14

Figure 17-15

Figure 17-16

Kathy Henjyoji designed and finger-knotted this choker, adding the interesting treatment of the beads with wire.

Beaded Wire Pansy, designed and worked by Arlene Baker. This pansy is made in the method used for beaded wire flowers from the nineteenth century.

Twisted square wire adds detail to wire and bead projects. Brooch designed and constructed by Cheryl Council.

Lapis and gold-filled wire bracelet, designed and constructed by Cheryl Council.

This dancing figure, by Cheryl Council, shows how a few beads and some wire can be transformed into a familiar image.

Chapter 18

Mosaics

osaics use small pieces of color to create a picture or design; most beadwork is actually mosaic by definition. This chapter looks at a few ways to design with beads using glue, rather than thread.

It's not a new technique; the Huichol Indians of Mexico have been making such mosaics for years using beads for colored tile and beeswax for glue. They lay the beads into the wax coated on an armature carved out of wood in a magical animal shape, or inside a gourd, so the holes face upward like a doughnut. They arrange the beads tightly together, so they create a hexagonal grid. The Star Christmas Ornament and the Mosaic Beaded Lampshade projects use these elements of embedding beads in an adhesive to create beaded mosaics.

Contemporary Huichol beaded lizard.

Star Christmas Ornament

You Will Need

3-1/2-inch papier mâché star
Tacky glue
Toothpicks
5 grams each or 1/4 oz. each of size 15 seed

beads in blue and silver
5 grams or 1/4 oz. of size 11 seed beads in
silver

This project takes the idea of placing beads with the hole facing up from the Huichol Indians. It takes some planning. Without the Huichol technique of keeping the beads in line in a hexagonal grid, it's easy to end up with gaps where a bead won't quite fit. So, as you glue the beads down, you need to think about the spaces you are leaving and whether a bead will fit between the others. The spirals used in this project are a perfect practice piece for learning how to plan your bead placement. If you start in the middle of a spiral, remember to leave a space for each color so the two colors of beads can wind around each other. You can also incorporate the year or your name, or use traditional seasonal motifs, to decorate the star.

Finished size: 3 inches

1. Squeeze a thin line of glue along two edges of the star. Rub the tip of a toothpick in beeswax or the glue, just to make it tacky enough to pick up a bead. Using the toothpick, place the size 11 silver beads in the glue along the edge of the star (**Figure 18-1**). Let dry, then glue another section of the size 11 beads along the edge of the star until all of the edges are lined and dry.

2. Begin a spiral pattern at the center of the star. Squeeze a pea-sized drop of glue on the star. Smooth to about a 1/16 inch thick, making a round glue section about the size of a penny. Using the toothpick as in Step 1, begin making a spiral of silver beads with blue beads as the background. See **Figure 18-2** for the beginning placement.

3. When one spiral is complete, surround it closely with blue beads and begin another spiral starting at the outer edge of the spiral and working in to the center (**Figure 18-3**).

4. Continue adding new glue sections as you fill in current ones. Take time to stop and look at the spirals and vary the direction and size, placing a silver bead in large blue gaps, building the design as you go.

5. Repeat the design on the other side of the star, or use a design of your choosing.

Figure 18-1

Figure 18-2

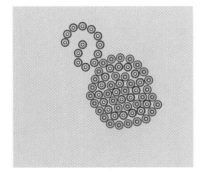

Figure 18-3

Meandering Vine Beaded Lampshade

You Will Need

Table lamp or candle lamp with a glass shade   One hank of size 11 green seed beads
Tacky glue   Pencil

Another way to glue with beads is to keep them in strands while placing them into glue and then sliding the thread out from the beads. This helps you keep the beads in a tight line, with all of the beads on their sides, and create flowing linear patterns with the beads. This project uses this technique with beads from the Czech Republic, which are packaged in hanks.

Finished size: Varies according to lampshade

1. Transfer the design (**Figure 18-4**) lightly onto the outside of the glass shade with the pencil.

2. Squeeze a line of glue along the vine and carefully place the beads on the line as close together as possible. Slide the thread from the beads in the glue. Let dry.

3. Squeeze glue in one leaf area at a time and place the beads, laying them in directionally (by holding a section of beads on the shade and draping them to the shape of the leaf's edge), as in the project photo. Repeat until all of the leaves are covered in beads. Let dry.

Figure 18-4

Chapter 19
Sampler Project

—————————————————— *You Will Need* ——————————————————
(for top section of design, described by use)

Base fabric: Cream-colored 28 count even-weave fabric 14 inches by 20 inches
House: DMC six-strand cotton floss # 712 cream
Roof and fence: 1/16-inch brown suede
Door and windows: DMC pearl cotton size 8, #415 silver gray
Tree trunk: Rainbow Gallery Pebbly Perle brown
Tree leaves: Needle Necessities Spring II,
#372 green
Tree leaves and background hills: Impressions by Caron, #208 Meadow
Hills and plants: Leah's hand-dyed size 12 pearl cotton, # 215 and # 217
Flowers: Size 15 rose, lavender, and white seed beads
Bead embroidery needle
Size 24 and 26 needlepoint needle
Needlework frame and stand

This project combines many of the techniques in this book, pulling from the samples described in the technique sections. The Beadwork Sampler design chart shows the layout and references where each technique is found in the book.

Finished size: 12 inches by 18 inches

To cross stitch the design:

1. Follow the House design chart. Begin with the house. Match up the center of the fabric, 4 inches below the top selvage, with the mark on the design chart. Using two strands of the cream floss, cross stitch the house, using a laying tool so the threads lie flat and parallel to each other.

2. Stitch the roof and fence using the brown suede and size 24 needle, following the stitching lines on the design chart.

3. Stitch the tree trunk and tree. Note that the stitching lines for the leaves are a mix of a half cross stitch over one or two threads in a random design.

4. Stitch the background hills with half cross stitches.

5. Stitch the branches to the rose bushes and foxgloves, then add the beads, using one strand of the cream floss and the bead embroidery needle.

To complete the Sampler:

1. Use the Beadwork Sampler design chart to make each sample. Arrange them below the cross stitch design according to the layout in the design chart or in your own arrangement.

2. Blind stitch in place.

3. Place the Sampler in a frame, being careful to have a space between the glass and the finished piece so that it will not be crushed.

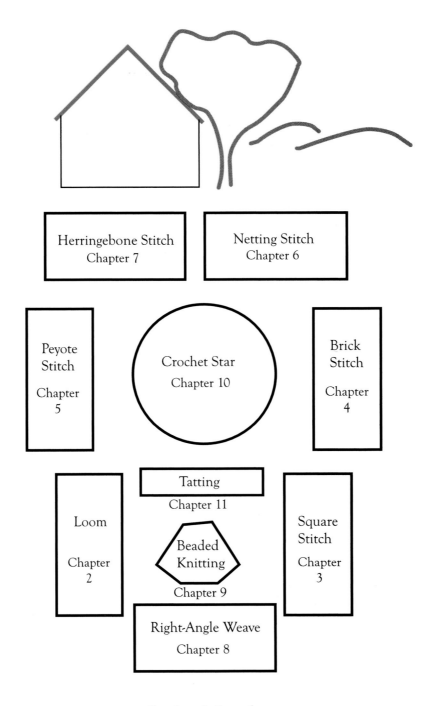

Herringebone Stitch
Chapter 7

Netting Stitch
Chapter 6

Peyote
Stitch

Chapter
5

Crochet Star
Chapter 10

Brick
Stitch

Chapter
4

Tatting
Chapter 11

Loom

Chapter
2

Beaded
Knitting

Chapter 9

Square
Stitch
Chapter
3

Right-Angle Weave
Chapter 8

Beadwork Sampler
design chart

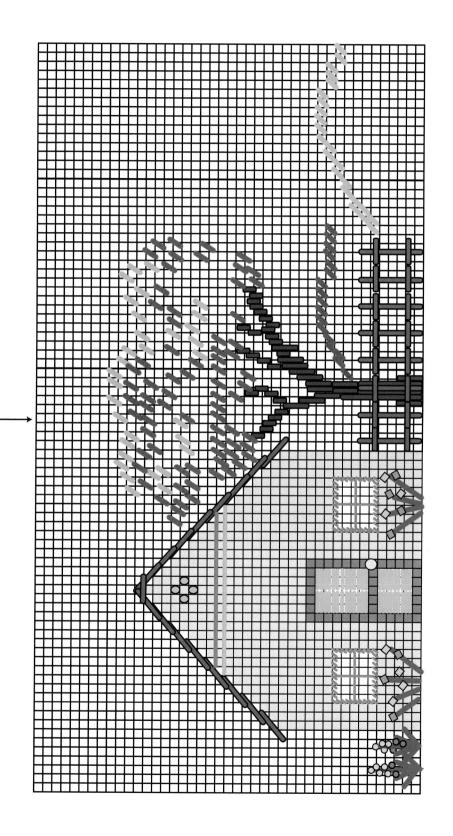

House
design chart

Graph Papers

Here are blank graphs for all of the graphed techniques in this book. In my opinion, this is one of the most valuable sections of this book, because you now have a resource to create your own designs. Many of the stitches, such as herringbone and right-angle weave, have not been used for patterns as extensively as peyote and brick stitch in most books, and this is the first printing of graph paper for these techniques. Just copy them, color them in, and enjoy!

Loom and Square Stitch Graph

Brick and Peyote Graph

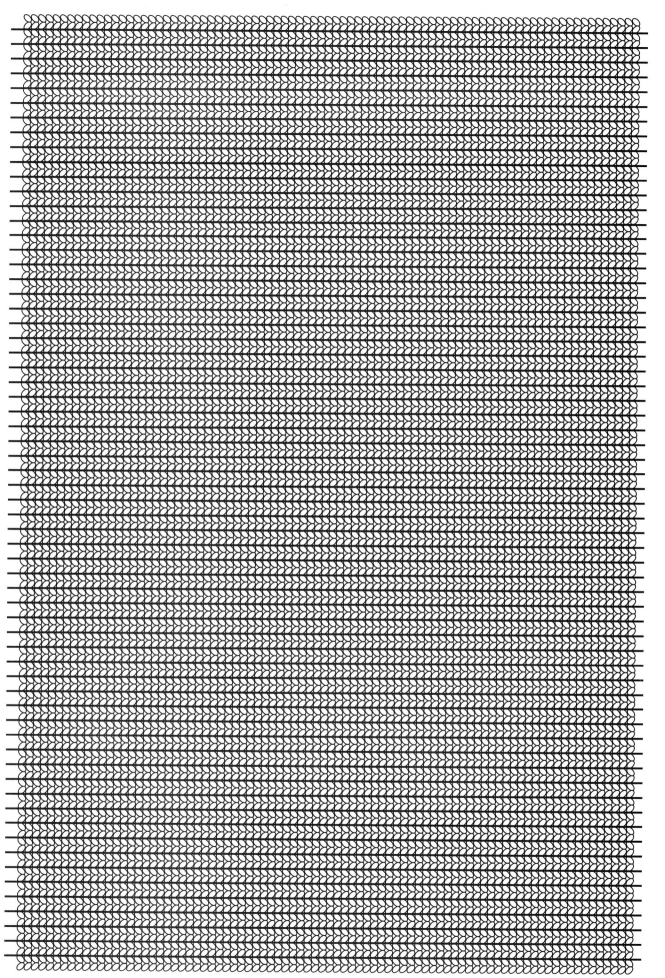

Herringbone Graph

Five Bead Netting Graph

Right-Angle Weave Graph

Bead Knitting Graph

Two-Drop Peyote Graph

Ladybug Brick Stitch Graph
(project on page 36)

Blank graph to cover 2" pumpkin box (Ladybug box)

Supply Sources

Whenever possible, I encourage you to seek out local sources for your supplies. Local stores need to be supported so they can continue to provide the valuable opportunity for us to peruse through their stock in person. This is something that can't compare to mail order; however, if you are unable to find supplies locally, here are some mail-order sources for products in this book.

Beadcats
Universal Synergetics Inc. Bead Store
P.O. Box 2840
Wilsonville, OR 97070-2840
(503) 625-2323
Fax: (503) 625-4329
www.beadcats.com
Owned by Carol Perrenoud and Virginia Blakelock, two of the first bead artists in this current interest of beading, this is a wonderful mail-order source, and the catalog is an information resource in itself about beads.

Blue Sky Alpacas
P.O. Box 387
St. Francis, MN 55070
(763) 753-5815
www.blueskyalpaca.com
My pattern for the bead knitted scarf on page 73 is distributed by Blue Sky Alpacas. The web page lists retail stores which carry the company's yarns and patterns.

Caravan Beads, Inc.
449 Forest Ave.
Portland, ME 04101
(800) 230-8941
Fax: (207) 874-2664
www.caravanbeads.com
Home of the Miyuki Delica Challenge—the bead contest that gave me the courage to pursue beading as a career—this is a great bead source for Miyuki products, from size 15 seed beads and Delicas to the large size 6 seed beads and triangles.

Creative Castle
2321 Michael Dr.
Newbury Park, CA 91320
(805) 499-1377
www.creativecastle.com
This store carries beads, beads, and more beads, as well as wire, findings, tools, and basic supplies for all things bead-wise. It also carries the wood bases for the napkin rings, salt and pepper shakers, and pumpkin boxes used for projects in this book.

Handy Hands
577 N. 1800 E
Paxton, IL 60957
(217) 379-3802
Fax (800) 617-8626
www.hhtatting.com
e-mail: tatthands@aol.com
This is the mail-order source for all things tatting. The company also carries several brands of cotton cord which are wonderful for bead crochet. Definitely worth looking into.

Weavers Needle and Frame
1610-2 Newbury Road
Newbury Park, CA 91320
(805) 499-7979
e-mail: weavlady@gte.net
Here you'll find all of the needlepoint and cross stitch supplies for this book, including Sudberry House wood products. Also does custom framing.

Artists in This Book

Arlene Baker

Arlene is an artist and teacher of Victorian ribbon and beadwork. She gets inspiration and learns techniques for her designs by studying her large collection of Victorian-era ribbon and beadwork. You can call Arlene to find out about her classes and kits at (562) 928-3583 in Downey, California.

Designs on pages: 132

Cheryl Council

Cheryl formerly worked as a designer in the aerospace industry. She is now a jewelry designer and teacher of wire jewelry making techniques. Cheryl has won numerous competitions, both local and in the state of California, with her artistic creations.

Designs on pages: 120, 126, 133

Marcia DeCosta and Linda Parker

Marcia and Linda teach under the name of MarLin Beads. They have been bead partners for the last six years and share a passion for beadwork and an enthusiasm for instructing others. Many of their pieces are inspired through collaboration, with each bringing their own unique design and color perspective to the finished work.

Designs on pages: 20, 44, 56, 65

Idele Gilbert

Idele Gilbert is an off-loom bead artist, designer, and teacher. She is currently creating original, three-dimensional designs in beadwork. In her pre-bead life, she was a needlepoint designer, miniaturist, and needle artist/teacher. She also is a mola maker and a designer of pop-up card patterns for rubber stampers.

Designs on pages: 41

Elizabeth Gourley

Elizabeth is co-author of *Art of Seed Beading* (Sterling Publishing, 1999). She loves writing, painting, doing all forms of needle art, and creating miniatures. She is currently working with her sister on a miniatures beading book. When she isn't beading, Elizabeth tends to her many animals and spends time with her family.

Designs on pages: 44

Kathy Henjyoji

Kathy loves to "fiddle" and has taught herself a lot. Her designs usually include a couple of different jewelry-making techniques. A dancer with a business degree, she works and teaches at Creative Castle in Newbury Park. Kathy also manages her husband's auto brokerage HARDYmotorsports and performs with costumes she has designed and made for Ajiva Dance Theatre in the Ventura County, California, area.

Designs on pages: 126, 132

Susan Hilyar

Susan is a nationally known teacher and bead artist. She is the publisher of *A River Flows*, a beadwork newsletter. Her work is shown in galleries and is frequently featured in *Bead and Button Magazine*.

Designs on pages: 64

Corinne Loomer

Corinne teaches beading classes and collects antique beadwork. She has won awards for her needlework and is always inspired by new techniques.

Designs on pages: 10

Dorianne and Shonna Neuhart

Dorianne and Shonna are a mother and daughter team of avid bead artists who began beading in the late 1990s. They have sold their work in boutiques and create custom orders of beaded jewelry. You can see their current pieces on display on their web page at www.ebetterbeads.com.

Designs on pages: 42, 56

Sylvia Sur

A lifelong interest in needlework and sewing led Sylvia to beads around 1994 when the popularity of beads had started to grow. "I enjoy the process of design and invention as much as wearing or displaying the product. I have learned a lot about using color in beads, which is the hardest part of learning to bead. Colors in glass do not act the same way as they do in paint, fiber, or fabric." When not beading, she designs websites and climbs mountains. Her work is on changing display at: http://home.att.net/~ssur/home.htp

Designs on pages: 20, 43

Carole Tripp

Carole creates designs for a line of bead kits and has had her designs published in several books. She teaches beading classes and is an avid promoter of beadwork, hosting a bi-weekly bead night at her store, Creative Castle, in Newbury Park, California. When not beading, Carole enjoys all types of needlework, softball, and spending time with her family.

Designs on pages: 42, 43, 113

Delinda Vannebrightyn Amura

Delinda is a nationally known instructor, whose work is shown in galleries and museum collections, including several pieces in the beadwork collection at the Smithsonian. She strives to incorporate antique techniques, workmanship, and materials into her intricate designs. She has a line of beadwork kits and imports silk thread for beadwork which can be found on her web page, www.delinda-v-amura.net.

Designs on pages: 19, 57, 114

Bibliography

Amura, Delinda Vannebrightyn. *The Illuminated Beading Manuscripts Book II The Loom*. Taos, New Mexico: Fairy Wing Press, 1997.
Delinda has presented more information on loomwork in this book than in any other loomwork book I have seen.

Barth, Georg. *Native American Beadwork*. Stevens Point, Wisconsin: R. Schneider Publishers. 1993.
Contains detailed information on peyote stitch.

Blumqvist, Gun and Elwy Persson. *Tatting Patterns and Design*. Mineola, New York: Dover. 1988.
This book shows clear illustrations for shuttle tatting and presents a large selection of patterns, though none include beads. It was originally published in Swedish in 1967.

Borjay, Genevieve. *The Basics of Bead Stringing*. Santa Monica, California: Borjay Press. 1998.
This is an excellent book on the basics of bead stringing with straightforward, clear illustrations and instructions.

Davis, Jane. *Beaded Boxes*. Ventura, California: Davis Designs Press. 1998.
This book presents several methods for using strands of beads to cover the same pumpkin boxes as in the brick stitch ladybug box (see page 36).

———— *Bead Netted Patterns*, Ventura, California: Davis Designs Press, 1999.
Here you will find more patterns in bead netting, including instructions for Odin's Glory on page 56 and Hollyhocks on page 57.

Foster, Barbara. *Needle Tatting Book I and Book II*. Paxton, Illinois: Barbara Foster. 1995.
These two little books were written by the owner of Handy Hands; I learned how to needle tat from them. Both have clear, simple photos and instructions.

Gourley, Elizabeth, Jane Davis, and Ellen Talbott. *Art of Seed Beading*. New York, New York: Sterling Publishing Co., Inc. 1999.
This book has information about many techniques for working with beads, including a photo step-by-step and 30 projects to make.

Korach, Alice. *Bead and Button Magazine*. Norwalk, Connecticut: Conterie Press. April, 1994 No. 2, pps 22 and 23.
Alice Korach, editor of *Bead and Button Magazine*, describes in detail her method of bead knitting, which is the technique I use for all of my bead knitting.

Paludan, Lis. *Crochet History and Technique*. Loveland, Colorado: Interweave Press, 1995.
This is an excellent resource of crochet history and styles. It includes a small section on bead crochet.

Reader's Digest. *Complete Guide to Needlework*. Pleasantville, New York: The Reader's Digest Association, Inc. Fifth printing. 1981.
I learned how to knit and crochet from this book after my mother taught me how to cast on. There are also sections on tatting, needlepoint, embroidery, and quilting, all of which are informative, even if the projects are dated.

Sanders, Julia E. *Tatting Patterns*. New York, New York: Dover Publications. 1977.
This is a wonderful reprint of a 1915 tatting book, showing unusual treatments for tatting, including several projects using beads.

Stessin, Nicolette. *Beaded Amulet Purses*. Seattle, Washington: Beadworld Publishing, 1995.
David Chatt's right-angle weave amulet bag is on the cover of this book.

Wells, Carol Wilcox. *Creative Bead Weaving*. Asheville, North Carolina: Lark Books. 1996.
This has become the standard for learning beading stitches such as peyote, brick, square, and right-angle weave stitches.

Glossary

Accent bead: A bead larger than other beads in a project, often with an unusual shape, color, or pattern used to contrast from the rest of the project.

African Helix Stitch: A spiraling beading stitch in which strands of beads are stitched together by passing around the thread of a strand on a previous round.

Antique bead: A bead more than 90 to 100 years old. Also, the brand name of cylindrical beads made by the Toho company of Japan.

Aventurine: A green semi-precious stone resembling green jade.

Bead: Anything with a hole for stringing or threading.

Bead crochet: Crocheting with beads strung onto the crochet thread and slid into the crochetwork as it progresses.

Bead fabric: A piece of beadwork.

Bead knitting: Knitting with beads strung onto the knitting thread and slid into stitches as they are made.

Bead knitting: Stringing beads onto silk or nylon cord and tying overhand knots between the beads.

Beaded knotting: Knitting with beads strung onto the knitting thread and sliding beads between stitches.

Beading needle: Needles made especially for beadwork which are longer and more slender than sewing needles. Some are made from twisted wire with a collapsible eye.

Blocking: To wet a finished piece of needlework, arrange it into the desired finished shape, and let it dry. This "sets" the threads in the piece, improving the overall appearance. You can also steam block by pressing with a hot iron at the steam setting.

Brick stitch: A beading stitch in which the beads are sewn together so that they resemble a brick wall.

Bugle bead: A bead shaped like a long tube.

Cabochon: A stone ground and polished so that the underside is flat and the topside is smooth and domed.

Charlotte: A round bead with a facet ground on one side. These beads sparkle in beadwork.

Comanche stitch: Another name for brick stitch.

Cone bead: A bead shaped like a cone.

Cross stitch: An embroidery technique in which colored threads are stitched in an "x" pattern on evenly woven fabric.

Delica: The brand name of cylindrical beads made by the Miyuki company of Japan.

Denier: A unit of measure used for silk thread.

Drop bead: A bead which is wider at one end. The hole can be through the length of the center of the bead or at the small end, perpendicular to the bead.

Facet: A flat section ground onto the side of a bead. Beads can have one or more facets. Charlottes have one facet, three-cuts have many random facets, and Swarvorski Crystals have precision-cut facets, like a diamond.

Finding: Components for making jewelry, usually metallic, including clasps, earring parts, pins, and jump rings.

Fringe: Long strands of beads along the edge of a project.

Gourd stitch: Another name for peyote stitch.

Hank: A number of strands of beads (usually twelve strands, each 20 inches long), folded in half with the ends tied together.

Herringbone stitch: A beading stitch in which the beads are sewn together so that they make a texture resembling the chevrons in herringbone fabric. Also known as Ndebele (pronounced en-d-Bell-ee) stitch after the Ndebele tribe of Africa which invented the stitch and uses it extensively.

Huichol (pronounced WEE-chul) Beadwork: A beading technique in which beads are pressed into warm beeswax, which has been coated on a wooden form or inside a dried gourd. This technique was invented and is used extensively by the Huichol Indians of Mexico.

Ladder stitch: A beading stitch used often as the first row in brick stitch in which a row of beads is sewn together, one bead on top of the other, resembling a ladder.

Lampwork bead: A bead made individually by melting glass and forming the bead on a rod using a small torch.

Leather needle: A needle with the sides near the pointed end ground flat on three sides so the needle can pierce through leather.

Loomwork: A type of beadwork in which beads are woven together on a loom.

Mosaic: An image created by using small colored components glued or drawn on a surface.

Needlepoint: An embroidery technique in which colored yarn or thread is sewn in a pattern onto a canvas.

Ndebele stitch: Another name for herringbone stitch.

Netting stitch: A beading stitch in which strands of beads, usually three or more, are sewn together in a loose fabric resembling a net.

Nymo: The brand name for a synthetic beading thread.

Peyote stitch: A beading stitch in which beads are stitched in an undulating pattern. Peyote stitch turned on its side looks just like brick stitch.

Picot: In tatting, a loop of thread between stitches. Sometimes beads are slid into the picots.

Right-angle weave: A beading stitch in which beads are sewn at right angles to each other.

Seed bead: A bead which is round like a doughnut and small. Seed beads range in size from the tiny sand-sized antique size 24 to the almost 1/4-inch size 5.

Shuttle: In tatting, a shuttle is the device which holds the thread as your work.

Spacer bead: A flat disk-shaped bead usually used as a decorative element in bead stringing.

Square stitch: A beading stitch in which beads are sewn together in regular rows and columns. Square stitch looks the same as loomwork.

Stranding: A beading technique in which strands of beads are manipulated to create jewelry or to decorate surfaces.

Tambourwork: An embroidery stitch in which beads are strung onto thread and a hooked needle fastened into a wooden handle (called a tambour needle) is used to make chain stitches on fabric as beads are slid into the stitches underneath the fabric.

Tatting: A lace making technique in which beads are strung onto thread and the thread is made into lace by making a series of half knots called half hitches, and beads are slid between stitches or into loops of thread. Tatting can be done with a tatting needle or a shuttle.

Tatting needle: A long blunt needle with a large eye used in tatting.

Triangle beads: Beads shaped like a triangle as seen looking through the hole.

Ultra Suede: A synthetic fabric made to feel like suede, but is easier to cut and sew through.

Vintage bead: A bead which is no longer manufactured but is not old enough to be an antique.

Warp: The vertical threads stretched on a loom which beads are then stitched between.

Weft: The thread which is threaded with a needle, then strung with beads and woven perpendicular to the warp threads on the loom.

Woof: Another name for weft.

Wirework: Bending wire into creative designs, including jewelry and decorative items, in which beads are often added.

Index